If All I Had to Do Was Coach

An Anecdotal Look at the Life and Times of a Longtime Coach

Brad Hackett

© 2014 Coaches Choice. All rights reserved. Printed in the United States.

No part of this book may be reproduced, stored in a retrieval system or transmitted, in any form or by any means, electronic, mechanical, photocopying, recording, or otherwise, without the prior permission of Coaches Choice.

ISBN: 978-1-60679-283-4
Library of Congress Control Number: 2013948003
Book layout: Cheery Sugabo
Cover design: Cheery Sugabo
Front and back cover photos: David Bracetty

Coaches Choice
P.O. Box 1828
Monterey, CA 93942
www.coacheschoice.com

Dedication

Thanks to all the coaches and athletes I've worked for and with over my almost four decades in track and field. This book wouldn't be possible without you. To my parents, the most influential coaches I ever had. And to my wife, Lorie, you were the inspiration to finish this book. Thank you all—I couldn't have done this without you.

Acknowledgments

There are almost an infinite number of people without whom this book wouldn't have been possible. I'd like to thank the following people.

My parents, Donald and Marjorie Hackett, you taught me right from wrong at a very young age, and Dad, you taught me the value of sports—a lasting lesson.

My high school track and cross-country coaches, Gene Primavera, Warren DeFrank, and Jerry Bielizna—thank you for a successful and exciting introduction to track and cross country.

My college coach, Jan Hunsinger—I couldn't have asked for a kinder and more caring college coach and thank you so much for giving me my start as a coach. I wouldn't be here today if you hadn't given me the chance. Bucknell University head coach Art Gulden, you taught me almost everything I know about being a college coach. The education I received from you in my three years as your assistant was priceless. Dick Coleman, head coach at Syracuse, you gave me the knowledge to become a head coach. Thank you for your willingness to trust me with many administrative duties.

I'd also like to thank all the assistant coaches and athletes I worked with over the years. Thanks for the memories.

There are also many people who read this book in its many phases and I'd like to thank all who read the book and gave me advice along the way, especially my brother David and my sister Joan.

Others who read the book and gave advice who I'd like to thank: Kelly Sullivan, Tom Amico, Tom Cartelli, Peter Moore, Scott Love, Mike Bruckner, Scott Bruce, and Jack Davis.

Finally, thanks to Muhlenberg College for hiring me as their head track coach. I had no idea when I started here that I'd found my home

Contents

Dedication 3

Acknowledgments 4

Preface 6

Chapter 1: Where I've Coached 13

Chapter 2: Kids Will Be Kids 19

Chapter 3: Characters 29

Chapter 4: Drug Testing and NCAA Rules 37

Chapter 5: Recruiting 45

Chapter 6: Vans 53

Chapter 7: Motels 73

Chapter 8: Towns 83

Chapter 9: Equipment 101

Chapter 10: Meets 111

Chapter 11: Facilities 119

Chapter 12: Camps, Clinics, and T-Shirts: Any Way to Make an Extra Buck 127

Chapter 13: The Blizzard of 1993 ... and the Roof That Came Down 137

Epilogue 145

About the Author 146

Preface

When I first started coaching more than 28 years ago, I had the grandiose plan of becoming the head track and field coach at a school in either the Pacific-10 (as it was then) or the Southeastern Conference by the time I was 40. After serving as an assistant track coach at three different Division I schools over a 15-year period and then a little over a year working in athletic equipment sales and now in my 15th year as a head coach at the Division III level, that rather naive objective of a young adult seems like a distance memory.

My coaching career has led me down an incredibly windy path, and on more occasions than I care to count, I've been confronted with crossroads and have had to make decisions as to which direction to turn. I've never once regretted the decisions I've made regarding the direction this path has led me, as I've encountered a myriad of wonderful experiences along the way.

I've coached All-America athletes, I've coached conference championship teams, and I've served as a member of coaching staffs for USA national teams. Therefore, I can comfortably say I've enjoyed a successful career in my chosen sport. Somewhere along the way, though—and I can't identify when or where this epiphany occurred—I realized coaching involves more than winning and losing. I'm an educator and the track is my classroom. If the team is successful—and believe me, I want the team to be successful—that's great, but what's most important is that the members of my team learn about life and mature into young adults when they're in my care.

Certainly, we all look back fondly on successful seasons, but ultimately, it's the day-to-day grind, the amusing people, and the infrequent and unusual experiences that break up the daily monotony that we eventually look back on years later and laugh about. When I first started coaching, I was always really serious. I wanted everything to go perfectly all the time, and whenever something did go wrong, I'd get very upset about it. It took me years to finally realize that the situations I got the most upset about at the time evolved into the things that I laughed about the most when looking back.

It finally occurred to me that these hiccups—these frustrating situations that eventually evolve into amusing anecdotes—are the journey. This is the path I've chosen, and if I'm willing to remain open minded, I'll realize that the more frustrating the situation is at the time, the more likely it is that the experience will evolve years later into a memory that will make me smile.

An Example

Early on in my tenure as an assistant with the track and field program at Syracuse University, I coached a pole vaulter named Steve. Steve was a wonderful young man and very creative and talented student, but he was also quite adept at keeping secrets. Steve was an industrial design major, and by the time he graduated from college, he already had several patents, including one for a lightweight wheelchair for handicapped children and another for a waterproof radio for boats. He was a genuine guy who liked to have fun and was always in a good mood, but his evasive nature was eventually going to cause a problem for our track and field program.

He'd pole vaulted all through high school and had a series of mishaps along the way—several of which led to serious injuries. Apparently, one time while in high school, he missed the pit when landing and broke his collarbone, and another time, his hand caught in the pole vault standards during a vault and he lost the last joint of his left pinky, as it was ripped off his hand during the jump. I'd eventually find out during Steve's junior year of college that at the end of his junior year of high school, his parents told him they no longer thought it was a good idea for him to pole vault, as he'd been hurt one too many times for them to continue to be sympathetic about his pursuit of pole vaulting and they forbade him from continuing with track. So, he ended up not participating on the track team his senior year of high school, and in his parents' eyes, his track career was over.

Despite his parents' ultimatum, Steve did come out for our team his freshman year of college and proceeded to have some great results. He earned a varsity letter his freshman and sophomore years and was really a positive and outgoing member of our team. He grew up in the Boston area, and during his junior year, we were scheduled to compete at Harvard University. I mentioned to him the week of the meet that I looked forward to finally having the opportunity to meet his parents when they came to see him compete that weekend in Cambridge. "Coach, my parents have no idea I've been on the track team for the last two-and-a-half years. They told me more than three years ago that I was forbidden from pole vaulting ever again," he said. My jaw dropped as I thought: "Your parents don't know you're on the team? Most kids' parents are really proud of their son or daughter's athletic prowess, but your parents don't even know you're doing this." Now that's my definition of evasive!

At Syracuse, the track team had three or four high jump and pole vault pits, and when they weren't in use, we stored these pits in a rather large cage behind the bleachers in Manley Field House. Manley was originally built in the 1960s as an indoor football practice facility and has a circumference of exactly 100 yards. At some point in the 1970s, Manley was converted from a football practice facility into a 10,000-seat basketball complex with a 200-meter track around the perimeter. When the bleachers were pushed in, there were hallways behind them on either side of the building. One hallway led to the locker rooms, training room, and weight room and the other hallway led to nothing other than exit doors for those sitting on that side of the arena during basketball games. It was behind the "leading to nowhere" side of the bleachers where we stored our pits.

The pits were stored in a cage that in my estimation must have been about 20 feet wide, 20 feet deep, and at least 20 feet high. It had a large swinging gate on the front that we could open and close when we brought the mats in and the gate also enabled us to lock the cage when the pits were inside so the local kids wouldn't get in there and climb all over them and potentially get hurt. The only people who'd any need to know the combination to the padlock were the coaches, the pole vaulters, and the high jumpers, for no one else ever had a reason to use the mats.

One year, during about the third week of school, one of the building's custodians mentioned to me that there was something a little odd about the pit cage. "Every day, when I walk by there, the pits seem as if they've been moved a little bit, but I never see anyone in there. It's getting to the point where I think I'm losing my mind, but I'm convinced there's someone living in there," he concluded. So, one night after I'd stayed in the office to make recruiting calls, I decided to take a walk down to the field house and investigate the situation for myself. The building had already been locked up for the night and the only lights that were on were the emergency lights. As I walked into the field house, I saw Steve, our friendly pole vaulter, walking out of the shower and back toward the pit cage.

I quietly walked over to the cage a minute or two later and scared the living hell out of Steve by asking, "Would you mind telling me what you're doing back here?" "Coach," he told me, "I have to admit I've been living in the cage for the past week or two. I bought a used car with the rent money my parents sent me, so I can't afford to move into my apartment until the beginning of next month. It's pretty easy to do. I just make sure I get into the field house every night before it closes and then sneak out first thing in the morning when it opens back up. It really isn't a bad place to live and the pits are really comfortable to sleep on."

That was a new one on me and I told him that he better call one of his friends and find a place other than the field house to live before he was able to move into his apartment. He readily agreed that living in the field house wasn't the smartest thing he'd ever done, but "Hey, I got a car out of it, didn't I?" he stated rather proudly.

It would be a funny little story if it had ended right there, but as luck would have it, the story didn't end with Steve moving out of the pit cage. One of our athletic administrators found out about it and reported it to our internal NCAA compliance director and the compliance director immediately reported this incident to the NCAA, as he determined this was an NCAA violation. The athlete wasn't on an athletic scholarship, and because he'd been living for free in an athletic facility, it was interpreted that he was receiving free housing from the athletic department. Therefore, it was surmised that Steve was on a partial athletic scholarship and thus we as a track program had gone over our maximum allotment of athletic scholarships.

Steve was then immediately suspended from the team until he either paid back the school for living in the pit cage or we as a track program declared him a scholarship athlete. A sport is only allowed a certain number of athletic scholarships—12.5 in men's track and field—and because we were already at the maximum, declaring him as a scholarship athlete wasn't an option. Finally, after more than three years as a member of our track team, Steve had to come clean with his parents, tell them he'd been on the track team for the past several years, and also ask them for some money in order to pay the school for the two weeks of rent he'd incurred by living in the pit cage.

Ridiculous, I know, but this is a classic example of what a college coach deals with on a daily basis. It's quite remarkable, oftentimes frustrating, and in retrospect frequently rather humorous the situations that young college-aged adults find themselves in, and far too often, their immediate response is to come running to the coach. I can't tell you how often I've sat in my office and listened to a sobbing athlete tell me his most recent predicament and thought to myself, "What does this have to do with track and field if all I had to do was coach?"

The Premise

"If all I had to do was coach." This seems to be the motto of every college coach I've ever met. No matter the age, level, ability, or sport, the position of coach has evolved into far more than the old stereotypical gym teacher that we all had growing up: the baggy gray sweats, a whistle around the neck, and a booming voice. An experienced coach wears almost an infinite number of hats, including social worker, psychologist, guidance counselor, bus driver, equipment manager, shoe salesman, travel agent, and surrogate parent. The perception that a coach walks out onto the playing field each afternoon, coaches the team, and then heads home for a burger and a beer is as far from accurate as assuming that Leonardo da Vinci was just an artist. Accept it or not, a coach's job entails an infinite number of facets—just as da Vinci's career encompassed far more than strictly artwork.

I've spent well over half of my life and all my adult life working in athletics. I've worked at three different NCAA Division I schools and one Division III school and have been a salesman for an athletic equipment company. I attended Colgate University, a small Division I liberal arts college in central New York, and remained at Colgate for two years after graduating as an assistant track coach. In 1985, I moved to Bucknell University and in 1988 to Syracuse University. I left Syracuse in 1997 to chase the American dream of earning big money and moved to Rhode Island to work for an athletic equipment company. Within a very short period of time, I realized I desperately wanted to get back onto a college campus, and in 1999, I moved to my present position as head coach at Muhlenberg College in Pennsylvania.

Throughout these years in sports, I've witnessed numerous incredible athletic achievements and many outstanding physical specimens and have had the opportunity to be associated with a plethora of wonderful human beings. This chronicle isn't about any of the aforementioned performances or individuals. It's a documentation of the lighter and often bizarre side of collegiate athletics—the experiences a coach encounters off the playing field and, in my opinion, the experiences that ultimately define one as a person.

My coaching career has taken me to four distinctly different schools, which has opened my eyes to many different philosophies and attitude toward athletic competition and the role of athletics on college campuses. But despite the differences, college students nationwide are basically identical. The questions they ask, the problems that confront their lives, and their maturation into adulthood are common denominators universally.

Although my college coaching career has remained entirely on the East Coast and therefore hasn't moved a great deal geographically, I've certainly traversed the entire spectrum of college athletics between the four different schools where I've coached. Colgate and Bucknell are rather small, highly academic institutions, trying desperately to compete at the Division I level, although I've never been certain whether those two schools are succeeding in their Division I aspirations. But when I was coaching at Syracuse University, we were hitting on all cylinders, as the football team was annually playing in major bowl games, the basketball team was playing in front of home crowds of more than 24,000, and the lacrosse team was also operating in the black and winning national championships on a pretty frequent basis.

I took a 180-degree turn going from Syracuse to Muhlenberg, as Muhlenberg is a small, private liberal arts college competing at the Division III level in athletics. I've oftentimes told people that the difference between Division I and Division III is this: "Monday through Friday are exactly the same. The difference is the level of athletic performance on Saturday."

Certainly, many other differences exist in the level of athletic participation at the four schools where I've worked, but many similarities also exist within the framework of what I've been exposed to. No matter what the level of an athletic program is, college students are college students and coaches are coaches. The way they act, the problems they encounter, and essentially what makes them tick are a constant no matter what the level of competition.

Unfortunately, life isn't a Utopianistic state and Murphy's Law—"Anything that can go wrong will go wrong"—seems to dictate life more often than not. Athletes encounter many unusual situations in their day-to-day lives, and therefore, the coach is also exposed to some quite intriguing, sometimes humorous, but more often than not rather frustrating situations.

It's these bizarre, unique, humorous, and head-scratching encounters that I'd like to share with you. Whether it's vans being driven in an ice storm, the team staying in a condemned hotel, or, my favorite, hosting the high school national championships in the Carrier Dome and having to let the roof down because of a blizzard, these anecdotes are funny, bizarre, and often frustrating, but hopefully after reading this chronicle, you'll understand why I frequently find myself mumbling in frustration "If all I had to do was coach," but then I look back on the same situation years later and laugh about it.

1

Where I've Coached

I've coached at four different colleges during my career: Colgate University, Bucknell University, Syracuse University, and Muhlenberg College. Not only are the four schools very different from one another athletically, but they're also quite different regarding their geographic settings. Colgate and Bucknell are in very small towns, but Syracuse and Muhlenberg are in medium-sized cities. For readers to fully appreciate the environments in which I've worked, I thought it would be appropriate to give at least a little bit of a description about each of the schools and the communities where I've lived.

Colgate University
(Hamilton, New York)

Upon graduation from college, I moved to New York City—as every red-blooded Colgate grad does—to seek my fortune and fame in the Big Apple. Within a few months of unsuccessful job interviews, too many rewritten resumes, and far too many subway rides, I realized that success in New York City wasn't in the cards. My college coach was gracious and daring enough (or possibly just desperate enough for help) to allow me to return to Colgate to assist him with his duties as the cross-country and track coach. Thus, my coaching career unceremoniously started due to my failure and, retrospectively, my lackluster and inept attempt to get my big break in New York.

I remained at Colgate for two years as a part-time track coach, making ends meet any way I could, including substitute teaching in the local school district, checking IDs at fraternity parties for $40 a night and all the beer I could drink—a great job for a 23-year-old—teaching physical education classes, and, of course, painting houses—the always-popular summer gig. Anything and everything to supplement the meager salary a part-time track coach directly out of college normally earns.

Colgate is in Hamilton, New York, about 40 miles from Utica and an hour drive from Syracuse. The town has a population of about 2,000 people—divided equally between university employees and farmers. Not exactly the kind of community in which a young postgraduate adult can anticipate a thriving and exciting social life.

A big night out for the coaching staff at Colgate was to head up to Pratts Hollow—a one-horse town about 10 miles up the road from Hamilton. At the single stop sign in Pratts Hollow was a church, a post office, and a bar called Coon Rods. Coon Rods may be the most unique drinking establishment I've ever had the pleasure of entering. The bar filled the first floor of owner Butch's home. The bar didn't have a ceiling—just parachutes and flags hanging from the rafters. The focal point was a jukebox that didn't require any money or have a single album recorded after 1972. All the draft beer was served in Mason jars and the bar had such wonderful games as pool, bumper pool, foosball, darts, shuffleboard and board bowling—the perfect environment for a coach looking for a little relaxing competition.

A Franklin stove dominated the room, as it sat directly in the center of the room and was surrounded by barbershop and dentist chairs and log stumps for foot rests. Coon Rods was known throughout the area for two things: the bipartisan men's room and Coon Dogs. The bathroom was filled with "intellectual" graffiti equally critical of both the Republican and Democratic Parties and a Coon Dog was some sort of red meat that I'm sure no biologist in the nation could decipher the ingredients of. To have the pure essence of a Coon Dog, one had to add a touch of Butch's special Coon Sauce—a combination of mustard and nuclear waste. The taste was incredible, and if the sauce didn't clean out your insides, it certainly could be used to clean off the bar's floor at the end of a busy Friday night.

Butch was about the nicest barkeep one will ever run into. Frequently, he'd tire of the excitement of serving beer in Mason jars and cooking Coon Dogs and let everyone know he was going upstairs to bed. He'd never throw his patrons out. He'd just ask that we serve ourselves, place our money in a jar, turn off the lights on our way out, and make sure the door was locked when we left. Now that's a bartender!

Bucknell University
(Lewisburg, Pennsylvania)

One could only take so much of such an enchanting social life as hanging around Coon Rods, and after spending four years there as an undergraduate and an additional two years as a coach, I was more than overdue for a change of venues. In the summer of 1985, I moved to Bucknell University—again as an assistant track coach—as the men's and women's jump, sprint, and hurdle coach.

Bucknell is in Lewisburg, Pennsylvania, about an hour north of Harrisburg and an hour east of State College. With it being three times the population of Hamilton, I certainly hadn't moved to the big city. Lewisburg has two primary sources of employment: the university, with an undergraduate enrollment of a little more than 3,000, and the maximum-security Lewisburg Federal Penitentiary (the former home of Jimmy Hoffa). A unique combination of employment prospects for the locals, to say the least, but surprisingly enough, I was never aware of any problems between the two institutions and I'm not sure the entire student body was even aware of the hardened criminals residing just a few miles to the north of campus.

My fondest memory of the athletic department at Bucknell has to be the annual senior awards ceremony. Christy Mathewson was a member of the very first class inducted into the Baseball Hall of Fame and a graduate of Bucknell and is certainly the school's most well-known athletic alum. The Christy Mathewson Award is given annually to the best male and best female athletes in the senior class. Not only is it a beautiful award with a great deal of history named after one of the greatest in the storied and long history of America's pastime, but the athletic director always contacts the winning student's parents and has them present at the dinner. Each year, two deserving athletes are excited enough in learning about receiving the award and then are even more surprised at learning their parents had been hiding in the back of the room to share in the occasion. This was truly a memorable moment each year and one I'll never forget.

Syracuse University
(Syracuse, New York)

My three years at Bucknell were an extremely grand learning experience, as I was given my first taste of a successful track and field program. Our cross-country team placed in the top 20 in the NCAA Men's Division I Championship two out of the three years I worked there and I began to discover I truly loved the sports of cross country and track and field and what a wonderful and joyous experience it was to work with dedicated athletes. After three years there, though, I once again had the yearning to move on, and in the summer of 1988, I was offered the position of men's and women's assistant track coach at Syracuse University, with the responsibility of coaching the jumping events.

If Bucknell was my introduction to successful college athletics and the beginning of the development of my awareness of my passion for coaching track and field, then Syracuse University was clearly my introduction to the big time of the college athletic community. It was the realization that college athletics is far more than an extracurricular activity and can indeed be a major business and a distinct source of revenue for the university in general and the athletic department specifically and also to the local community's economy. The Big East Conference, the Carrier Dome, the largest on campus athletic facility in the nation, top 20 football (bear in mind, this is the late 1980s and early 1990s), top 10 basketball—Syracuse was the epitome of big-time college athletics in the 1990s.

As a community, the city was absolutely obsessed with the university's athletic department. With snow on the ground a rather large percentage of the year—believe me, some years, it seemed like the majority of the year—I think the university's athletic teams served as a great divergence for the citizens of the area, and oftentimes, it appeared as if the people of the town lived and died by whether the football, basketball, and lacrosse teams won or lost.

The Carrier Dome serves as home for the Syracuse football, basketball, and lacrosse teams. The facility holds 50,000 for football and lacrosse and has on several occasions held more than 30,000 for basketball. Over the years, many interesting characters have set foot in the dome during home contests.

The Dome Ranger was a middle-aged local disc jockey dressed up in an orange cowboy outfit who ran the sidelines of the basketball court for years. He had to retire, though, after it became too demanding to run up and down the court after every basket when the team started scoring in the 100s on a relatively consistent basis. Dome Eddie, a man who for many a season came to every home contest dressed from head to toe in orange, including an orange wig, was another Carrier character, but his consistent attendance ended abruptly when after a heartbreaking defeat, he was trampled on the dome floor by disappointed students and broke his leg. The Dome Knitter used to attend every home basketball game dressed in all orange and sat quietly during the games knitting orange mittens. The aforementioned three personalities certainly characterize the communities' obsession and dedication to their beloved Orangemen.

I'd be remiss when describing Syracuse if I left out what may be its most unique landmark: Onondaga Lake. A mile wide and six miles long, this former part of the Erie Canal is totally polluted. For years, the local steel company and every other merchant on its borders dumped everything and anything into the lake to the point that no one may now set foot in the water. It has been said that if the lake were dredged of all its waste, the entire city would be covered by six feet of toxic waste. Millions of taxpayers' dollars have been spent over the years to try to figure out a way to clean up the lake, but unfortunately, no simple or logical cleanup project ever has been established.

Muhlenberg College
(Allentown, Pennsylvania)

I moved to Allentown, which is located in eastern Pennsylvania in the Lehigh Valley, in the fall of 1999 and have been here ever since. Muhlenberg is a small liberal arts college with a great academic reputation. I felt almost immediately that I'd returned to my roots. Although Muhlenberg is an NCAA Division III athletic program and all the other schools where I'd coached were Division I, Muhlenberg is very similar academically, athletically, and sizewise to Colgate and Bucknell.

Billy Joel once wrote a song entitled "Allentown," a song really written about Bethlehem, Pennsylvania, a neighboring city to Allentown. Bethlehem Steel was at one time the second-largest manufacturer of steel in the nation and during World War II employed almost half-a-million people. During the 1960s and 1970s, "The Steel" fell on hard times, and to this day, the former employees blame the management and the former management blames the unions for the demise of the company. Whoever was ultimately at fault, Bethlehem Steel eventually went bankrupt.

Joel's song was written to draw attention to the plight of the out of work steel plant employees, but he was unable to write lyrics that rhymed with Bethlehem, so he wrote it using the word *Allentown* instead. Therefore, for years, many in America had an inaccurate perception of Allentown based on a song that in reality wasn't even about the city.

As an undergraduate and as a coach at Bucknell and Colgate, I frequently competed against Lafayette College and Lehigh University—two other schools located in the Lehigh Valley. We must have stayed in rundown hotels when we competed against those schools, as my initial perception of the Lehigh Valley prior to moving here was quite negative. Based on those hotel experiences and Joel's song, I was under the impression I was moving to a former down-and-out northeast industrial city that had fallen on economic hard times. Thankfully, my first impressions were inaccurate, as Lehigh Valley in general and Allentown specifically is a wonderful place to live.

Let's Get on With It

Now that you have a better idea as to where I've lived and coached and now that you're aware I've desperately tried to put a positive and humorous twist on some rather frustrating situations, let's get on with it. What follows are some of the stories that have shaped my path.

2

Kids Will Be Kids

One thing I'm quite confident in stating is that college-aged students are incredibly unpredictable. They're frequently quite gullible and always of the opinion that if they heard something on a college campus, it must be gospel. Oftentimes, their actions can be very frustrating. Sometimes, they can say or do something that's downright precious, and almost always, they think the world revolves around 18- to 22-year-olds. Most of the time, this isn't their fault, though, as life on a college campus is quite insular and living in the college environment is a grand maturation opportunity with almost an endless safety net.

Nevertheless, college kids never cease to amaze me with their actions and the unbelievable predicaments they can burrow themselves into. Helping athletes dig themselves out from these self-induced holes is oftentimes gratifying, sometimes educational, and very often eye opening. Parents tell their teenage children they were teenagers once and that anything their children can dream up, they also thought about many years previously. Believe me, if parents only knew, they'd be stunned at some of the things their kids are capable of.

You've Gained How Much?

Many people assume that to be a great thrower an athlete has to be as big as possible. Size, as with anything else, certainly has a point of diminishing returns. One year along my coaching path, I was coaching at a school that had a really, really good female thrower. She was clearly blessed with a gun for a right arm and was also fortunate to have really fast feet—a great combination for any thrower.

One year, she qualified for the NCAA Championship and returned home at the end of the meet as an All-American. I don't recall what place she earned, but I do remember she did very well, although she was beaten by a couple different throwers from another school that has had a great tradition in track and field for years. At that point, the school's throws coach had been as successful as any throws coach in the country. That next summer, a track and field publication ran a story about the great success the throwers from that school had had at the meet, and one of the athletes was quoted in the article as saying the reason she improved from not making the finals the previous year to winning her event that year was due to the fact that her coach had encouraged her to gain 15 to 20 pounds of muscle during the off-season.

What the athlete didn't say, though, was that she was six feet tall and only 160 pounds during the year that she didn't make the finals and had gained the suggested 15 pounds to become a still relatively svelte six feet, 175 pounds the year she earned her gold medal.

Our thrower, who was probably 5'9" and 220 pounds, read the article, and without any conversations with her coach, she made the assumption that if the other school's coach thinks that 15 to 20 pounds helped his thrower, then it certainly will help her.

But she didn't stop at 15 pounds, as she returned to school the next year weighing at least 250 pounds and totally lost any foot speed she'd possessed the year before. She did the exact opposite of her counterpart, as she went from placing at the NCAA Championship to not making the finals the next year.

No matter how hard coaches try to stay on top of their athletes and their training between seasons, sometimes a coach can do nothing, as the athletes are capable of rationalizing things that no adult would ever contemplate as being logical. Her coach couldn't do anything for her and all was lost from one misinterpretation of a quote in a magazine.

You Got Lapped!

Whether I was coaching at Colgate, Bucknell, or Syracuse, for years, I made the long journey to Williamsburg, Virginia, the first weekend in April for the Colonial Relays at the College of William & Mary. It's a beautiful campus in a wonderful town but a really long drive, as it's a seven-hour drive from Bucknell and at least 10 from Colgate and Syracuse. By the time I started coaching at Syracuse, the buses were all equipped with VCRs, so the kids would always bring a variety of movies to pass the time, but 10 hours on a bus is still a long trip. We always departed campus on Thursday morning, arrived in Williamsburg late in the afternoon, competed Friday and Saturday, and then immediately got back on the bus when the meet was over and drove through the night to arrive home early Sunday morning.

One year at the Colonial Relays, a blind man entered in the 10,000 meters (10K). A 10K is a little more than six miles or 25 laps on a standard 400-meter outdoor track. No matter how you slice it, a 10K is a long race on a track. When a blind athlete enters a middle-distance or distance event on a track, he's allowed to run alongside a guide. The guide holds a string that's also attached to the right wrist of the blind athlete, although the guide must always stay slightly behind the competitor so as not to be accused of pacing the athlete. In a race as long as the 10K, the blind athlete may also have several guides who may switch on and off during the course of the race.

In this particular 10K race at William & Mary, we also had an athlete entered in the race. Our runner wasn't a great athlete and we didn't expect him to fare very well. The blind athlete ended up breaking the world record for a blind 10K, and in the midst of his successful race, he lapped our athlete not once but twice, as our runner finished several minutes behind the leaders.

On the way home on the bus, one of our athletes placed Eddie Murphy's standup routine movie Raw in the VCR. Raw is rather crude, has a great deal of swearing in it, and can be tough for even the crudest of us to watch without cringing at least a few times. At one point during the movie, our 10K runner stood up and demanded that the movie be turned off, as he believed the film was too offensive for some on the bus.

From the back of the bus came out a cry I'll never forget: "Yo, Stevo, you got lapped twice by a blind guy. You got no right to demand anything. Now sit down and shut up." The entire bus exploded with laughter and poor Stevo spent the rest of the bus trip in silence. Kids can be tough on their teammates.

Where's Your Luggage?

Sometimes, it's not the parents who did the spoiling but rather coaches all the way from youth leagues through high school and on to college and in some cases the pros. Many successful football players also run track in the spring and there have always been several football players on the track team wherever I've coached. The difference in the experience for an athlete playing football and running track at the Division I level can be quite significant, as one sport tends to fly to away contests and play in front of tens of thousands of fans, whereas the other sport competes in front of a few members of the immediate family and travels by van.

I do think the track experience for many is as much if not more gratifying because the athlete is competing for himself and dramatically less pressure is involved. There can indeed be clashes of the two different cultures, though, or at the very least misunderstandings.

One year, we were heading out to the airport to fly to the USA National Championships in Los Angeles and one of the members of our team making the trip was a football player. We loaded up the van at the field house and one of the members of our department drove us out to the airport. The kids grabbed their bags out of the back of the van, walked up to the counter, checked in, received their tickets, and proceeded through airport security out to the gate. Twenty to 30 minutes had passed since we got out of the van, and as we were sitting at the gate waiting to board our plane, the football player said, "Hey, which one of you do I need to thank for grabbing my bag and checking it in for me?" We all looked at each other rather oddly and asked, "What makes you think any of us took your bag?" "Well," he responded, "during the football season, the equipment managers put all our bags under the plane for us. I didn't grab my bag. I thought someone else would do it for me."

I called back to campus and asked the person who'd taken us to the airport to go out to the van to see if any bags were in the back of the van. Sure enough, his bag was still sitting in the backseat. By the time our driver was able to turn around and go back to the airport with the bag, our flight had loaded and taken off without it. In the years before September 11, airport security was much less stringent than it is today and he was able to put the bag on the next flight out to Los Angeles, and when we reached our layover in Chicago, I called back to school and was informed by our airport chauffeur that the bag would reach the airport in Los Angeles five hours after our flight was due to land.

That afternoon was my first experience with LA traffic. We arrived at LAX around 4:30 p.m., and by the time we got our luggage and loaded up the van, it was probably 5:15 or 5:30. I don't remember the name of the highway, but we had to drive from LAX out to Walnut and it must have taken us two hours. Bumper to bumper the entire way. On the east coast, when you have traffic like that, you expect to see an accident, a fire or a broken-down car at some point to justify the frustrating traffic. Not the case in southern California. This, I was told, is a daily nuisance. To make matters worse, the entire time I was fighting the traffic, in the back of my mind, I knew I had to turn around and go back to the airport several hours later to pick up the football player's luggage.

We eventually arrived at our hotel, went to the track to do a workout, got something to eat, and then the football player and I got back in the van to the airport. "Gee," he said, "if someone had grabbed my bag in the first place, we wouldn't have to be going back to the airport now." I thought I was going to kill him. What stunned me then was that what had taken us two hours in one direction at 5 p.m. only took 45 minutes round-trip at 10 p.m. I don't know how people who live in Los Angeles can take that. We ended up getting the bag, going to Disneyland the next day, and having a successful meet, so all's well that ends well, but a difference certainly exists between football players and track athletes with regard to what they expect others to do for them.

She Bit You?

The Penn Relays is the oldest track meet in the United States. It dates back to 1895 and has been contested annually at the University of Pennsylvania in Philadelphia every year since then. The three-day meet is quite amazing, and if the weather is nice in the northeast on the last weekend in April (if being the primary word), up to 45,000 people will be in attendance daily. Schools come from all over the country to participate, and for many, it's the highlight of their season if not their careers to have the opportunity to compete.

The meet is filled with tradition, as many past, present, and future Olympians have blessed Franklin Field with fantastic performances. As a collegiate athlete in the 1960s, Bill Cosby competed for Temple University at the Penn Relays and still returns every year to entertain the crowd. It's a magnificent experience and truly is a carnival as well as a track meet. Many don't know this, but the first-ever telecast for ABC's *Wide World of Sports* was the Penn Relays.

We'd always leave campus on Wednesday afternoon after the kids got out of class and drive down to Philadelphia. For several years, I was fortunate to be working for a school that was allowed to stay at a hotel right across the street from the campus and within walking distance of the stadium. This meant our bus driver had a great gig, as once we unloaded the bus on Wednesday afternoon, he was free to do whatever he wanted until Saturday night and was on the clock the entire time. We certainly never saw him at the meet, so I'm sure he was out enjoying the sites of the city on our school's budget. On Saturday morning, the kids were instructed to put their luggage in the storage compartments under the bus and then meet us back at the bus when the meet was over to head home.

The bus had been stationary since Wednesday night and again Murphy's Law reared its ugly head: As soon as we were all on the bus and the bus driver went to start it up, of course it wouldn't turn over. The bus was parked right out in front of the hotel we'd been staying in all week, so we suggested that everyone head back into the lobby of the hotel and get something to eat while we waited. The bus driver called a local Philadelphia bus company and it said it would send someone over to fix our broken-down bus. We waited and waited and finally a couple hours after the bus driver called, a repairman arrived to fix the bus.

In the meantime, the kids were getting pretty antsy to get back home and were starting to fool around in the lobby of the hotel. A couple girls on the team decided they'd rather wait on the broken-down bus than sit in the lobby any longer and headed out to the empty bus. At some point a little while later, one of the guys on the team decided to go out to the bus to get his Walkman®. Unfortunately, an incident ensued on the bus that I'm sure we never really got to the bottom of.

Depending on whose side of the story you wanted to believe, it was apparent that the male went out to the bus and stepped over the two girls, who were lying across the aisle trying to sleep. He knocked one of them in the leg as he stepped over them, and according to him, he apologized, but according to the women, he didn't. Words were exchanged and the two women and the male began to wrestle on the bus. How or why I don't know, but at some point, the guy's ear was bitten severely enough that it warranted medical attention, including a tetanus shot.

While all this was going on, the repairman had fixed the bus and had walked into the lobby of the hotel to tell our bus driver we were ready to go. Out the front door of the lobby we went and onto what we thought was an empty bus—only to discover a fight between the three going on inside the bus. So, even with a repaired bus, we weren't able to head back to school, as we had to go to the hospital to have the male athlete's ear treated. This has got to be the epitome of kids will be kids, as a scenario like this would never happen with adults—well, other than with Mike Tyson.

Your Girlfriend Is What?

We had a really good freshman athlete one year—to whom we'd offered a tuition scholarship to entice him to enroll. His parents were very excited with the offer and agreed to be responsible for his room, board, books, and fees in exchange for our offering him a tuition scholarship. The athlete was from a rather small town and wasn't the most sophisticated person on the face of the earth, but he was a good kid and a great athlete.

I don't know how or why, but his high school girlfriend had a situation in her home life that led to her moving in with her boyfriend's parents when he went off to college. During the indoor season of his freshman year, this young man was doing really well, competing at an extremely high level and really impressing me with not only his ability but also his competitiveness. As the outdoor season progressed, though, his behavior and performances began to become somewhat erratic.

Initially, I assumed the erratic performances were due to his being a freshman and somewhat new to the sport, but I finally decided a week or two before our outdoor conference championship to ask if anything was wrong. "Coach," he said, "my girlfriend is seven months pregnant and I don't know what to do. My parents are really upset with me and are threatening to throw us both out of the house." I quickly counted backward seven months and concluded he'd gone home for fall break and gotten his girlfriend pregnant while she was living in his parents' house. Did he not know about birth control?

We finished the season and I brought the young man into the office and asked him what his intentions were for the following year. He assured me he'd resolved the problems with his parents and had already found an apartment for the following fall semester for his girlfriend, child, and himself. I didn't give it a second thought, as he seemed quite confident he had everything covered. I didn't know at the time, but I was about to have one interesting education.

The first day of school the following fall arrived and into my office walked our now-sophomore athlete. "Coach," he said "I want you to meet my wife." Wife? I had no idea he'd gotten married over the summer. After our introductions, he went on to inquire as to where he could pick up his rent check from the athletic department. I explained to him that we paid his tuition, not his rent. He seemed stunned, saying "I'm getting a tuition scholarship. Doesn't that mean you pay my room, board, books, tuition, and fees?" "No," I responded. "A tuition scholarship means we pay for your tuition. You pay for everything else."

"I didn't pay for anything last year" was his response and I said: "Yes, you're right. *You* didn't pay for anything last year. Your parents paid for your room, board, books, and fees." There was then an utter and complete silence from husband and wife as reality began to set in that they had no way to pay for their apartment. Finally: "My parents told me I was on my own since I'm now married, but I never realized they'd been paying for part of my education last year. I thought I was on scholarship. Now what am I supposed to do?"

I told them I'd make some phone calls and let them know what I could find out. I have to admit I had no idea what I was getting myself in for and didn't even have a starting point as to whom, what, or where I should go to get the answers to my yet-unrealized questions.

It took me several weeks of nonstop work, but I finally discovered that the baby and the mother were eligible for government-subsidized housing, although the athlete on my team wasn't because he was a full-time student. I also found out where mother and daughter needed to go to apply for WIC and food stamps. We were then able to find our athlete a part-time job at a fast-food restaurant to help defray the costs of the housing and the three of them were at least able to survive between the housing, the WIC, the food stamps, and the part-time job.

Shortly after we started practice, it was very obvious that going to school full time, taking care of a wife and child, working part time, and training for the upcoming track season was too much for the young man to handle. No sooner had he finally learned to adapt to the stresses from all the different directions he was being pulled than he walked into my office rather dejected one afternoon before practice to inform me that his wife was once again pregnant.

Now he had a wife, a child, another child on the way, a part-time job, full-time academics to study for, and the expectations of the coaching staff to attend practice every day to earn his tuition scholarship. Sadly, it was too much for him to handle and he had to drop out of school, therefore ending his potentially successful track career and, more importantly, his chance of earning a college degree. Some stories are funny, some are humorous, and some are sad. This one was just devastatingly disappointing on several different levels. No matter what we tried to do to help the young man, it was just never going to be enough.

You Were Sent Roses?

One year, we went out to the University of Oregon to the NCAA Championship in Eugene. Eugene is Mecca as far as track and field in the United States is concerned. The birthplace of Nike, this community has been supportive of track and field for many, many years. The track facility is magnificent, the running trails spectacular, and the local fans second to none regarding their support and knowledge of the sport.

While I was in Eugene one year for the NCAA Championship, I went into a local deli with a friend of mine who'd been quite successful during his own college career 20 or so years earlier. The middle-aged woman behind the counter kept on staring at us to the point where it was becoming a bit uncomfortable. Finally, she said, "Didn't you run 13.32 in the high hurdles for Southern Illinois back in 1981?" "Yes," he sheepishly replied. "I did." "Boy, I remember you were great out of the starting blocks," she went on to say. That's Eugene, Oregon. It's the only place in the country where track and field athletes learn what it must be like to be a professional football or baseball player walking the streets of the city where they play.

Early one morning, I heard a knock on my hotel room door and a local florist appeared with a dozen roses in his hand. He told me the front desk had informed him that I was a coach for Syracuse and that he had a delivery for one of our female athletes by the name of Susan. I took the flowers to Susan's room and she was just about in heaven when I handed her the gift, as she was nearly hyperventilating because she was so ecstatic. Later that day at the meet, Susan was downright giddy with all her teammates and it was quite clear to everyone on the team she had an admirer.

Our head coach was also pleased, as he certainly played the role on our staff of the surrogate parent for all the athletes on the team, and whenever one of the athletes was happy, he'd also be pleased, and whenever any of them were down, he'd also be down, as he was always the kind of person who wore his heart on his sleeve. The rest of the week in Eugene, our head coach couldn't stop talking about how happy he was for Susan, frequently mentioning he'd never seen her so happy and clearly it had something to do with the flowers she received.

After a while, for the rest of us, it became a bit much, as over and over again throughout the course of the week, she kept asking each of us if we'd seen the roses she'd been sent. The poor member of our team who'd been sharing a hotel room with her must have heard it 15 or 20 times.

Our coach was somewhat old school and was rather conservative in his background—politically, ethically, and morally—and I don't think it had ever occurred to him that the athlete's admirer wasn't a guy. When we got on the plane in Eugene to fly home, Susan asked our head coach if it was all right if her new friend picked her up at the airport and brought her back to campus rather than going back with us in the van from the airport. He even mentioned to us he was looking forward to meeting the young man who was clearly making Susan's life more enjoyable.

We arrived back in Syracuse and walked down to the baggage claim area to pick up our luggage and Susan's new friend was waiting for us. The two exchanged glances from across the room and sprinted toward each other and immediately embraced. Our coach looked as if he were a deer in the headlights, as he of course had no problem with the two women hugging. It was just that for several days, he had had an entirely different image in his mind and was utterly confused by this unexpected embrace.

He immediately went over and introduced himself and was just as happy as could be to meet Susan's new girlfriend, but I'll never forget the immediate and initial reaction—not based on disapproval but rather on how stunned someone can be when he encounters something he was anticipating for days that ended up being very different from his initial expectation.

You Don't Care if You Graduate?

Sometimes, the things we do can frustrate us in retrospect, whereas other things can sadden us and sometimes we can do things that please us. Once in a great while, we can do something that really makes us proud, and this is one of those things. I coached an athlete from an inner city, who was really gifted. He was also very street smart and had grown up in a relatively tough neighborhood and really knew how to take care of himself.

Every fall and spring semester around midterms, coaches will receive midterm grade reports on all the athletes on their teams. This particular athlete didn't do exceptionally well during the first half of his first semester in college. He'd befriended many of the guys on one of the other sports teams and was traveling in a rather fast-paced lifestyle with the athletes who were clearly the classic Big Men on Campus.

I brought him into the office after I'd received the grade report and had a heart-to-heart talk with him about his grades. I'll never forget his response to me when I expressed my concerns. "Yo, Coach, your job ain't to worry about me graduating. Your job is to make me a better athlete" is what he told me. "No, my job is to help you become a better athlete and to make sure you graduate on time" was my response. "My friends have shown me the tricks to stay eligible, so I promise I'll stay eligible, but I don't care if I graduate. Just worry about my results" was his final statement on the subject.

It took five years—sometimes getting along; sometimes at each other's throats—but he persevered and eventually graduated. He was quite successful as an athlete, but more important than that was that he ended up earning his degree and was going to be able to go out into the world with a college diploma.

The weekend of his graduation, I got a phone call from his grandmother. "You're the only man who has ever meant anything to my grandson and I want you to know how much I appreciate you standing by him," she said. I was speechless, as I'm sure tears were on the verge of running down my cheeks. No one had ever said anything nicer to me in my entire life and I've never felt the pride that I did at that particular moment. The five years of frustration and the constant badgering had paid a huge dividend. A phone call from an athlete's grandmother was the just reward.

Most of the time, the phrase "If all I had to do was coach" is used when complaining about a particularly bizarre experience, but once in a while, as with the preceding story, it's obvious that some parts of a coach's job that are above and beyond the coaching aspect are ultimately the most rewarding.

3
Characters

I've been very fortunate to have had a wonderful career coaching at some of the finest institutions of higher learning in the nation. I also spent a year and a half in sales and learned a great deal about the sport while selling track and field equipment. For many years, I was also involved with USA Track & Field, the sport's governing body in our country, in a variety of different volunteer capacities, including six years as the national triple jump chair for the men's development committee and for seven years as the overall men's development chair.

During my full-time job as well as serving in different volunteer capacities, I've had the good fortune of meeting many people who have been memorable for their athletic abilities, their personalities, their temperaments, or their ability to overcome huge obstacles—clearly far too many people to write about, but some have stood out for their unusual behavior or for saying or doing something so unique that it has stood out in my mind over time.

How Much Pie Is Too Much Pie?

Many coaches end up coaching in the same event area they competed in themselves as athletes, and throwing coaches are no exception to this frequent metamorphosis. Throwers are usually the largest members of any track team and subsequently throws coaches tend to also be large. We had a throws coach one year who used to joke as he patted himself on the belly: "Yep, yep, yep. I'm just a biscuit under 350 and I think I ate that biscuit this morning." He was a part-time coach and drove a donut delivery truck to earn extra money and would purposely slam on the brakes when driving the truck to force some of the boxes of donuts and cookies to fall on the truck floor, hoping a box might open and therefore not be allowed to be stocked on a store's shelves and hence allow him to eat the contents.

Throws coaches are often rather large human beings and therefore are capable of eating massive quantities of food. One time, we were staying in a hotel the night before our conference championship and I went out to dinner with our throws coach and our school photographer. We went to an Italian chain restaurant that had an option on the menu for all the salad, bread, and pasta you could eat. I had no doubt what our burly dining mate was going to order for dinner.

After eating several bowls of salad, an equally large quantity of bread, and several plates full of pasta, the waitress came over to ask if we'd like to order dessert. The photographer and I had already loosened our belt buckles to the very end and remarked to the waitress, "Who can order dessert after all that food?"

"I'd like to order dessert," our throws coach said. "What's on the menu?" The waitress said she'd be right back and returned a moment later with a plate loaded with seven different kinds of pie. I don't mean apple or cherry pie either. I'm talking about peanut butter chocolate death and seven-layer chocolate cake—really thick, heavy desserts that looked like they'd go right through the table if you dropped them.

The waitress proceeded to describe each kind of delicacy individually and our mate evolved into a version of Homer Simpson as he began to drool and moan as she continued to regale him with the various desserts. When she was done, he was utterly confused as to what to order. "Gee," he said. "They all sound so good. I don't know what to do." His indecisiveness continued for several minutes and the photographer finally put a $20 down on the table and said to the waitress: "Bring him one of each. I can't sit here all night waiting for him to decide."

She ended up bringing a plate to our table with seven different slices of pie on it and our buddy immediately began devouring the plate in front of him. He went through the first six slices as if it were nothing and then as he took the first bite of the seventh slice said: "Oh, this is far too rich. I don't know how anyone could eat this." Our photographer and I almost fell on the floor because we were laughing so hard. "Too rich?" we said almost in unison. "You just ate six pieces of pie. Of course it's too rich." That's one I'll never forget.

The Annual Birthday Bar Crawl

We annually hosted the Big East Indoor Track & Field Championships in the Carrier Dome while I was coaching at Syracuse. The meet was always the second-to-last weekend in February. (I always felt badly for the athletes from the University of Miami for having to leave South Beach to fly to Syracuse in February.) The meet was always on the same weekend as the birthday of one of the young assistant administrators in our department. For this story, we'll name him John.

John was an alumnus of Syracuse and many of his college fraternity brothers still lived in the area, so John and his college buddies still enjoyed heavily imbibing the "golden nectar of the gods." One of John's favorite sayings was "Beer is my friend." Each year on his birthday weekend, John would rent a bus, buy a keg of beer for the back of the bus, and invite his fraternity brothers and all the members of our department to tour 10 to 15 bars in town on his rented bus.

Sadly, I never had the opportunity to experience this endeavor due to the track meet, but I always heard some great stories. The annual bus trip always ended at the same Irish pub on the west side of Syracuse. At 2 a.m. when the bar closed, everyone would return to the bus and head home. At least, that was always the plan. One year, a young graduate student who worked in our department apparently went to the men's room right at closing time and passed out in a stall. The bus departed the Irish bar without realizing it was one person short, and amazingly enough, no employee at the bar bothered to check the bathrooms before closing.

Our young graduate student ended up waking up inside the bathroom around 5 a.m., had no idea where he was, and upon walking out of the bathroom realized he was locked inside a bar after closing. He accidentally set off the burglar alarm and remarkably enough was able to convince the police when they arrived that he wasn't trying to break into the bar but rather break out of the bar.

This young man's responsibility within our department was to work with the sports information office, covering the nonrevenue sports home contests. This meant that he had to be in the Carrier Dome at 7:30 a.m. to cover the all-day track meet. We all got a lot of mileage out of making fun of him that day, as he was certainly several shades of green, and on more than one occasion that day he had to go "pray to the porcelain gods."

Sometimes, I was envious of those who were able to partake in the annual barhopping bus trip, but after seeing that poor graduate student, I realized how fortunate I'd always been to have an excuse to miss the event.

Beauty Pageant

A few years ago, the NCAA Outdoor Championship was somewhere out in the Midwest and the host institution was a couple hours away from the nearest airport, so we'd decided that instead of staying in a hotel near the school the night after the last day of competition that we'd check out of our hotel before heading over to the meet and then drive the two hours back to the airport and find a place to stay near the airport at the conclusion of Saturday's competition.

When we arrived earlier in the week, I'd made a mental note of the hotels around the airport and called one of them midweek in order to make a reservation. I was successful in reserving rooms, and when we arrived early in the evening on Saturday night, we checked right into our hotel.

The hotel lobby was mobbed with little girls between the ages of six and eight and I didn't give it a second thought as we rode the elevator up to our rooms to shower and change before heading out to a local restaurant for dinner. When we came back down to go to dinner, the mob of young girls had changed from chaos into hundreds of Saturday morning cartoon–watching kids all dressed up as if they were on the verge of walking a runway at a fashion show in Paris.

I mean, these kids were dressed to the nines, but they were only little kids. Makeup, eye shadow, and lipstick with made-up hair that would make a high school prom queen envious. It was one of the most confusing things I'd ever seen, as these were little kids trying to look like adults. If that wasn't bizarre enough, the mothers were out of control. Following their daughters around the lobby putting on more makeup and using portable hair dryers for that last-ditch effort to make them look even more perfect. One mom was even hemming her daughter's dress in the lobby as the girl stood there in her underwear.

It was rather serene as these little kids were trying to look so mature but at the same time were on the verge of losing it, as they were so nervous. I have to admit I never even knew such an event existed and to see the money, time, and expectation being spent was incredibly extreme. The mothers were putting a great deal of pressure on these little kids. I was walking through the lobby with athletes who were returning from the NCAA Championship—young men and women who are great athletes and are used to competing under pressure—and they all agreed that these little kids looked as if they were under more pressure and stress than any of them had experienced at the track meet. It was truly an eye-opening experience for me and exposed me to a world I didn't even know existed.

He's Gone

We had an assistant coach one year who left in the middle of the school year right as our season was about to begin. He had a chronic bad back, and one day during practice, he was out throwing a football with some of the athletes he coached and he threw out his back for the umpteenth time. He went to see his chiropractor and the physician informed him that he really needed several weeks of bed rest to fix has ailing back.

Without telling a single member of the track coaching staff, he took the doctor's advice to an extreme level by packing all his belongings and moving back into his parents' house several hours away in another state. It didn't take long for us to realize we were missing a coach, although it did take several days to track him down. The athletic director came into our head coach's office and informed him that our now-missing assistant coach had filed for worker's compensation, as he was claiming that his injury was work related. So now, not only had he left without telling anyone he was leaving, but he was claiming that throwing a football around with his athletes was the cause of his injury, despite the fact that he had a pre-existing back problem.

The school had no choice but to honor his worker's compensation claim and he began to receive a percentage of his salary despite the fact he wasn't even in the same state. One of the lawyers for the worker's compensation insurance company decided to do a little research into the claim and went to the coach's hometown to investigate. Apparently, his parents owned some kind of retail store in his hometown, and when the attorney went to pay him a visit, he was actually working at his parents' store despite the fact he was claiming compensation for his inability to work.

The attorney informed him that his claim was then and there null and void because he was actually working when he was claiming he was incapacitated. The following fall when the school year began, he actually came back to our campus thinking he still had a job. The head coach naturally informed him that his job was no longer available, as he left the previous year in the middle of the season without telling anyone he was leaving. He was furious, screaming at our head coach about how unprofessional it was for the head coach to have given his job to someone else without even informing him. How ironic is that? Someone who didn't even have the decency to inform anyone that he was leaving and to then yell at the head coach for hiring someone else? It's tough sometimes when on that rare occasion you work with a coach who's less mature than the athletes.

Athletic Directors

An old maxim in academia says: "Those who can, do; those who can't, teach; and those who can't teach administrate." In coaching, the saying is "Athletes who can, do; coaches who can't coach administrate." This really isn't true, as most athletic administrators are dynamic individuals with the coaches' best interests as their primary priorities. Exceptions to every rule do exist, of course, including athletic directors.

I worked for an athletic director at one point in my career who'd been a college wrestling coach for the majority of his career. He went into athletic administration rather late in his career and wasn't exactly the sharpest tack in the box. The president of the college was fond of asking: "Wrestling? Are you sure he was a wrestler? I think his actions appear more like he's a punch-drunk boxer." Not exactly a resounding endorsement from one's superior.

I worked for another athletic director who really took school spirit to a new level. For the sake of this story, let's say the school's mascot was a bulldog and the school colors were red and blue. The athletic director had his wife order blue polyester with red bulldogs in the material as a pattern. She then had a three-piece suit made out of the material and he'd wear this obnoxious outfit to all the school's contests.

A local car dealership decided it would be great publicity for its business if it supplied the athletic department with a customized van. The van was blue with red trim, a bulldog on either side of the van, and another bulldog on the back of the van covering the spare tire. On the bottom runners on either side of the van in large red letters was written "This Is Bulldog Country." The dealership gave the van to the athletic department with the intent the coaches would use it when they went out on the road recruiting. This never happened, as the athletic director turned this gift into his everyday vehicle and the coaches in the department were never given the van for recruiting purposes.

As I mentioned earlier, the school mascot was a bulldog and the athletic department had a giant bulldog costume a student would always wear at the home athletic contests and its name was Billy the Bulldog. The athletic director's daughter was a student at the school while I was coaching there and ended up getting engaged to a fellow classmate. The family planned the wedding and reception for their daughter and she made the decision to wed in the school chapel. Most college chapels have weddings almost every weekend in the summer, and when planning a wedding, the chaplain's secretary is always a good source for suggestions for planning the big day with regard to such things as a florist, an organist, food preparation, and even local chauffeurs. The secretary suggested a local horse-drawn carriage company to transport the bride and groom from the wedding to the reception.

I wasn't invited to the wedding, but I was told afterward that the family declined on the horse-drawn carriage and had Billy the Bulldog drive the bride and groom from the wedding to the reception in the customized van emblazoned with "This Is Bulldog Country" and the father of the bride wore his polyester three-piece bulldog suit. I even heard rumors that instead of the father of the bride having the first dance with his daughter that Billy the Bulldog had the honor. That's just a rumor, but it wouldn't have surprised me.

The athletic director and I left the school the same year for new jobs. Several years later, I ran into the track coach from the athletic director's new school and I was told he was still driving the same customized van with Billy the Bulldog on the sides.

4

Drug Testing and NCAA Rules

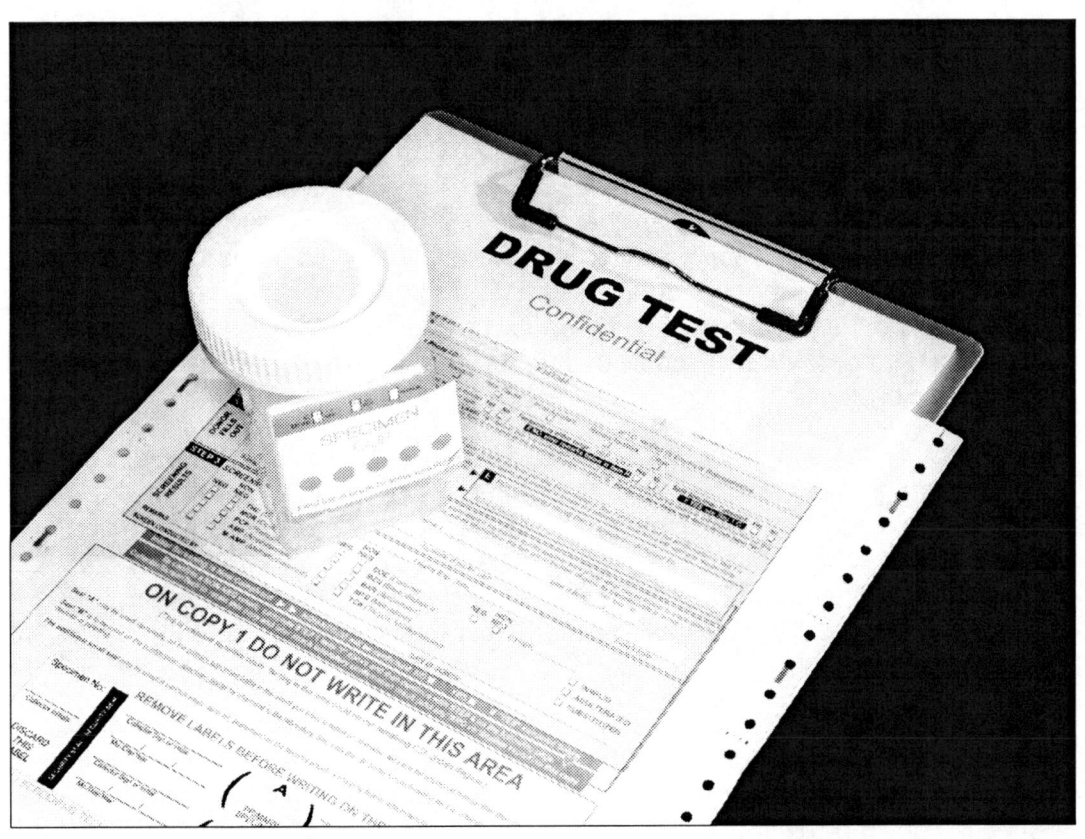

Clearly, certain aspects of any job really don't excite the participants in that particular field of employment. Learning the NCAA rulebook and becoming well versed in the policies of drug testing are two parts of a coach's job that most in the profession really don't enjoy very much.

The NCAA rulebook is almost as thick as the Bible and almost impossible to fully understand. It's entirely realistic to read the NCAA rulebook in an attempt to verify whether something is legal or illegal in the eyes of the NCAA and to find various rules interpretations within the book that confirm that a particular issue is simultaneously permissible and impermissible. Not only can the book be extremely confusing and contradictory, but sometimes, the rules just don't make sense.

Drug-testing rules and procedures can also be very confusing. In today's athletic environment, it's obviously necessary to test for drugs, but one unfortunate aspect of drug testing is absolutely no wiggle room exists within the rules and I think every coach has had at least one experience where he has just thought: "Come on—give me a break. This is just ridiculous." So, without further ado, what follows are a few examples of rules interpretations and drug-testing procedures that can leave a coach thinking: "Give me a break. If all I had to do was coach."

Is a Gold Medal Worth It?

Early in my career, a good friend of mine who was the swim coach at the same school where I was working was also a member of the U.S. women's water polo team. During the era of this story, women's water polo wasn't an Olympic sport, so the World Championships was without a doubt the most important competition for the sport. Without the opportunity to compete for an Olympic gold medal, the members of the national team trained and focused all their energy on one single objective: winning the World Championships.

The World Championships in this particular year was in Sydney, Australia, so the team departed from the west coast of the United States for a two-week training camp in Hawaii to prepare for their journey Down Under. During one of the practices in Hawaii a few days before the team was to depart for Sydney, my friend was elbowed in the mouth and her tooth broke off right at the gum line. Her roots were still intact—imbedded in her mouth—but the tooth itself was totally gone and probably sitting at the bottom of the pool.

In team sports, when a country wins a gold medal in an international competition, each and every member of that team is a candidate for drug testing. If one member of the team tests positive for a banned drug, then the team is disqualified and it loses its medal. For example, if a single member of the men's 4x100 meter relay in the Olympic Games tests positive, the other members of that relay don't get to keep their medals. The entire team is disqualified even though only one athlete tested positive.

Anyway, after my coaching peer was taken out of the pool and the bleeding was stopped, she was told she was going to need to have emergency root canal surgery immediately. The team doctor went with her to a local dentist and explained to her as they were driving to the doctor's office that she had an important decision to make right then and there. If she allowed the dentist to use anesthesia during the root canal surgery, it was entirely realistic that if she were tested for drugs during the World Championships that she could test positive and therefore jeopardize the entire team's chance at a gold medal. The team doctor went on to explain that if she chose to allow the dentist to use any kind of drugs during the root canal surgery, it would be the team doctor's recommendation to the head coach that she not be permitted to play during the World Championships.

So, there she was, driving from the pool to the dentist office—clearly in a great deal of pain and on the verge of a root canal—and she'd been told that either she can have the surgery without anesthesia and be allowed to play or have anesthesia and go home without ever having the opportunity to compete in the World Championships. Mind you, she'd been training for years for this once in a lifetime opportunity, so no surprise to any elite athlete, but she chose to have the surgery without anesthesia.

The team left Hawaii and arrived in Sydney and competed in the World Championships. Murphy's Law once again reared its ugly head and the team was upset in the semifinals and had to settle for the bronze medal, so none of the athletes underwent drug tests and therefore my friend needlessly suffered through an anesthesia-free root canal.

Drug Testing a World Record

When an athlete breaks a world record in track and field, he's subject to an immediate drug test or else the world record won't be ratified. The International Association of Athletics Federations (IAAF) is the international governing body of track and field and is responsible for such issues as the ratification of world records. A few years back, a friend of mine coached an athlete who broke the world record in an indoor middle-distance event at a collegiate track and field meet. The host school certainly wasn't prepared for an onslaught of a world-record attempts at their meet, so for obvious reasons, it hadn't made any preparations for postmeet drug testing.

At the conclusion of the meet, my friend called the American representative to the IAAF rules committee and asked what he needed to do for his athlete's world record to be ratified. He was told that because the meet didn't have the availability to test her for drugs on the spot, he had 24 hours to get her to a nationally sanctioned drug-testing lab and have her provide a specimen. The team loaded up its bus after the meet and went back to its campus while the coach spent the ride home making phone calls to verify the closest drug-testing lab.

He discovered they were going to have to go to New York City the following morning to provide the specimen, as New York was the closest site from their campus—about a 90-minute drive. Coach and athlete left first thing in the morning for New York—the athlete purposely not going to the bathroom before arriving in New York to ensure she had enough of a sample to satisfy the drug tester. She signed the forms, met with the doctor, and went into an adjacent room with a female observer and provided the required sample for the attendant and proceeded to empty her bladder into the toilet.

The doctor then walked into the room as the attendant was placing the top on the two jars filled with samples. The doctor immediately noticed the attendant didn't have surgical gloves on her hands, took the samples away from her, and poured them down the toilet, saying: "You've contaminated this sample by not putting gloves on. We can't use them." He turned to the athlete and asked if she could provide another sample, and she replied "No, I've just gone to the bathroom."

The doctor told her to go back to the waiting room, drink several bottles of water, and wait until she could go again. She did what she was asked to do, and an hour or two later, she said she was ready to provide another sample. She went back into the examination room with the same assistant. This time, the attendant had gloves on and the athlete provided another sample. The doctor came into the examination room after the sample was provided, held the jar up to the light, and exclaimed as he dumped the sample down the toilet: "You drank too much water in a short period of time. This sample is too clear. It's obviously just the water that has run through your system. We're going to need to try again."

By this time, coach and athlete were getting more than just a little upset. This time, the doctor told her to drink a variety of fluids and to go out for a run or some lunch to ensure the next sample would be acceptable. The athlete went out for a long run in Central Park, drank a large quantity of various nonalcoholic beverages, and ate lunch. She was finally able to provide another sample at around 4 p.m., nearly eight hours after initially arriving at the lab. Almost in tears at this point, she was praying the doctor would accept the sample. Fortunately, the doctor did accept the sample and athlete and coach were able to drive home.

Sadly, though, the very next weekend, at a large international meet in Europe, the world record was again broken, so my friend's athlete's world record never did have to be ratified because it was broken before the IAAF had the chance to recognize her performance. She spent an entire day providing samples for a record that never made it on the books.

Crohn's Disease and Athletics

Some stories are funny, some are incredibly stunning, some are ridiculous, and others are sad and unfortunate. This one is sad and frustrating. One of my stops along the way had an athlete on the team from another country. He was an incredible athlete and really had a realistic chance of earning a spot on his country's Olympic team.

When coaching an elite foreign athlete—or an elite American athlete for that matter—the coach not only needs to be aware of the NCAA rules regarding eligibility but also the athlete's national governing body's rules and regulations. If the athlete is a superstar, the coach also needs to be familiar with the IAAF and International Olympic Committee (IOC) rules and regulations. Although the coach needs to be aware of a variety of rules and regulations, when it comes to ensuring his athletes stay eligible to compete, it's imperative for the coach to know the drug-testing rules and what drugs are on the banned substances list. Different countries have different rules and these rules may or may not be the same as the NCAA.

Our entire coaching staff was really excited when this athlete decided to enroll in our school, as we knew he had the potential to not only be a school recordholder, conference champ, IC4A (Intercollegiate Association of Amateur Athletes of America) champ, and an NCAA All-American, but it was very obvious even when he was in high school that he had the tools to go all the way to the highest level in our sport. His freshman year didn't disappoint, as he won his event in our conference meet, placed at the IC4As, and made it to the NCAA Championship. Not bad for a freshman. We were satisfied we'd made the right decision in bringing him to our school.

Unfortunately, during his sophomore year, the performances didn't continue to improve and he began to look rather sluggish and not nearly as aggressive, fast, or powerful as during the previous year. Initially, we were chalking it up to the sophomore slump, but soon, it became apparent it was something much worse than a mythical excuse. He began to have a hard time eating and he was unable to keep weight on. So, after some initial consultations with our athletic trainers, it was determined that the athlete needed to see a specialist.

Within a very short period of time, the athlete was diagnosed with Crohn's disease, a disease of the intestines. I'm not a doctor and won't even attempt to describe the treatment, but my recollection is that the athlete needed to have either a part of his colon or lower intestine removed to prevent the disease from spreading. Once the surgery was successfully completed, the athlete had to be treated with a medication that included a steroid.

Prescribing a steroid for most patients with this disease is probably not an issue, but this young man had aspirations of earning a bid to the Olympic Games. We had to jump through myriad hoops to obtain permission for him to be treated. His nation's track and field federation, the IAAF, and the NCAA had to give permission before the doctors were able to prescribe the medication. It didn't take too long for all the various governing bodies to give their approval, and before very long, our ill athlete was able to begin his cycle of medication and get back on the road to recovery.

It took him several years to get back athletically to where he'd been pre–Crohn's disease, but it all worked out in the end. He competed for his country in the World Championships and the Olympic Games after he'd graduated from college. I guess the reason I say it was sad and frustrating is that his event-specific coach at our school had to go to great lengths to ensure not only the eligibility of the athlete, but more importantly, he had to go to extreme measures to enable this young man to be treated medically like anyone else with his condition would've been immediately in order to satisfy the regulations of various organizations.

Athletic Scholarships

Athletic scholarships are something frequently desired, oftentimes misunderstood, and far too often can get an athlete and a program in deep trouble. In team sports, such as football and basketball, the application of scholarship rules is pretty simple. The NCAA determines how many scholarships you're allowed to have in a particular sport and that's how many athletic aid packages the coach is permitted to award. For example, in football at the Division I level, the NCAA permits 85 scholarships per team. Therefore, 85 athletes on a football team earn an athletic scholarship.

I've been away from Division I long enough that the rules may have changed since I coached at that level, but when I was coaching in Division I, track was allowed 18 scholarships in women's track and 12.5 in men's track. The rules are different in football, though, as this doesn't mean you have 18 women and 12.5 men on scholarship, as the coach is allowed to divide the money up any way the staff chooses.

A full scholarship is determined to be the total value of what the school's financial aid office has estimated the combined costs of room, board, books, tuition, and fees to be. So, in women's track, for example, the coach takes the financial aid office's estimated cost of enrollment and multiplies that number by 18 to come up with the total dollar amount he's allowed to award in scholarship money on his team. The area where a program can get into a problem, though, is once you start dividing the scholarships in half, the athletes may not receive any aid from other sources.

If a women's track coach decided to award 36 half-scholarships or if a men's coach awarded 25 half-scholarships, none of those athletes can accept any financial aid from the institution outside of their athletic award. The reason is that once an athlete is given any athletic money, then all the money he or she is awarded from the school is considered athletically related funds. So, if a coach gave out 36 half-scholarships and if one of those 36 athletes received one penny of financial aid, the program would be in violation, as they'd have given out more than 18 full rides.

It certainly can be confusing and a coach has to do a great job of accounting for not only the awards he's handed out but also what—if anything—the athletes are receiving in outside aid. The coach not only needs to pay attention to the financial status of the athletes on the team who are receiving scholarships, but he must also be aware of the financial aid packages, work-study jobs, and hometown booster club scholarships the students not on scholarship are earning. The coach must do this for two reasons. If a nonscholarship athlete earns money during a work-study job in an athletically related facility, this money is determined to be athletically related and therefore that student's work-study money counts as scholarship money and then his entire financial aid package is considered an athletic scholarship. This is also the case if a nonscholarship incoming freshman has been awarded some money from his high school athletics booster club. All his money is then considered athletically related.

It can be almost impossible to keep track of all this and make sure a sport hasn't exceeded its allowable allotment of athletic scholarships takes a full time accountant, let alone a track coach to keep track of. Needless to say, problems arise all the time. Keeping track of this is a real pain in the neck.

We had a freshman on our team one year who before our first team meeting—where we'd explain all the rules—accepted a work-study job with our dining services working in its catering department. The catering services people assigned him to a concession stand in the Carrier Dome selling hot dogs at football games. The football, basketball, and lacrosse teams played in the Carrier Dome and it's therefore designated as an athletically related facility. Thus, any job in the Carrier Dome constitutes an athletically related financial award and all his financial aid was subsequently determined to be an athletic scholarship. So, by working four hours at $5 an hour selling hot dogs at a single football game, this freshman's entire financial aid package was now considered an athletic scholarship.

When this slight mistake was discovered a few weeks later, three alternatives were proposed for a solution. We could count his aid against our allotment of scholarships, which wasn't possible for two reasons: He wasn't a very good athlete and we were already at 12.5 full awards. The other two solutions were either he quit his job and return the $20 he earned that day selling hot dogs or he wouldn't be allowed to compete on the team. The freshman gave up his job, begrudgingly returned the money, and was then declared eligible to be on our team.

Selling hot dogs at football games wasn't the only ridiculous situation we ever encountered regarding nonscholarship athletes counting against our scholarship allotment when I was at Syracuse. We had an average triple jumper on our roster one year who'd received a $500 scholarship from his high school booster club during his senior year of high school. The scholarship was an annual gift awarded from his high school to the varsity athlete with the highest grade point average in his school. One could argue it was an academic award, as it was given to the student-athlete with the highest GPA in the school and that it was acceptable for him to keep the money. Our compliance office, though, deemed that because it was awarded by the booster club for the student-athlete with the highest GPA—*athlete* serving as the key word—this money and subsequently any financial aid he was receiving would count against us. So, just as with the student selling hot dogs at football games, this athlete had to make a similar decision: Send the booster club award back or quit the team. The student gave up the scholarship and was allowed to compete.

Sadly, students can't always afford to give up money in order to compete. We had a woman on our team one year who was unable to overcome her particular financial predicament. We discovered that her high school track coach also owned a track and field sporting goods store in her hometown. Annually, the coach would hire several of the athletes on his team to pose as models for his catalog. The athlete on our team was paid $250 to appear in his catalog wearing track and field warm-ups, uniforms, and running shoes. Because the catalogue was selling athletic equipment, the money earned for her modeling appearance was immediately deemed as athletically related, and as with the other two athletes, all her financial aid was determined to count against us. Just as with the other two scenarios, she had to make a decision: Return the money and be allowed to compete or keep the money and not compete in collegiate athletics. Unfortunately, she didn't have $250 available to her, so she had to quit the team.

The best example to describe what a ridiculous rule this is has to be lifeguards. A swimming pool is determined to be an athletically related facility if the school sponsors swimming as a varsity sport. One would have to assume that the members of a college swim team are the best swimmers in the school, but if the student-athlete isn't on scholarship and is receiving financial aid, then he can't serve as a lifeguard in the school's pool.

So, these are just a few examples of why a coach can sometimes become just a little bit irritated with rules. Of course, the NCAA and the various international governing bodies have rules in place for a reason, but it does indeed get a little frustrating once in a while, and the toughest situations are the ones where an innocent student-athlete is placed in a no-win situation, which is why we can all oftentimes be heard mumbling under our breath: "Give me a break. That's just ridiculous."

5
Recruiting

If drug testing and NCAA rules serve as the thorn in the side of many college coaches, then recruiting can serve as the rose. Frequently giving pleasure to a coach, but at the same time, recruiting may also have thorns. Nothing is more satisfying to a coach than spending many months recruiting a blue-chip athlete who commits to the coach's institution, but nothing is more frustrating than spending those same months on a recruit who eventually turns him down.

Every coach who has ever worked at the collegiate level has experienced a recruit telling him he's applied to schools A, B, and C, making the coach believe he has a legitimate chance of enrolling the athlete—only to have the student-athlete at the last minute tell the coach he's enrolling at school Z, an institution that was never even on anyone's radar. Nothing is more maddening than a recruit telling a coach that the student has narrowed his choice down to the coach's school and one other and then being told he's going to attend a third school he never mentioned in all the months of recruiting. It eventually makes the coach think he was never in the hunt in the first place.

Recruiting can be incredibly fickle and coaches end up being rejected far more often than they succeed. One has to have very thick skin to recruit, as rejection is the norm, not the exception, and it's very realistic for a coach to have to recruit 5 to 10 times as many athletes as he'd like to enroll in the incoming freshman class. But as most coaches would agree, recruiting is the name of the game, as the successful recruiter who has a talented team is going to beat the greatest coach on Earth who has little talent 9 out of 10 times.

So, whether or not a coach enjoys recruiting, it's certainly a necessary evil in the field of college coaching. The coach has to put the time into the process to be successful even if he's aware of the frequent frustrations that go hand in hand with the effort. The coach has to send out hundreds of recruiting forms and then weed through the ones that are sent back, determining who should and shouldn't be recruited. Ultimately, it boils down to this: A coach's eventual success depends on the college choices of 17- and 18-year-old kids.

Weeding Out

The first objective a coach has when the recruiting forms are mailed or emailed back from the recruits is to determine whether he should recruit the athlete. Sometimes, that process is very easy. Every recruiting form has basic information requests on it: name, address, telephone number, birthday, etc. The forms also request such academic information as grade point average, SAT or ACT scores, and class rank. Even though the coach's first inclination is to look at the athlete's best performances on the recruiting form, the academic information is ultimately the primary factor as to whether the athlete should be recruited.

The best athlete on the planet can't and shouldn't be recruited if the athlete doesn't meet the school's admissions office's academic requirements. Nothing is more frustrating than putting months and months into the recruiting of an athlete and then find out that the admissions office isn't going to accept the student. So, the weeding out process is imperative to the coach spending his recruiting time wisely and putting in his effort on athletes who have a legitimate chance of being admitted.

Every recruiting form I've ever sent out as a coach has had a line on it that requests "SAT Scores _____." I've certainly always expected that the athletes were aware of what that's requesting and I've always utilized this information in my weeding out process. One year, I received a recruiting form back from a recruit with a question written on this line: "What are Saturday Scores?" Needless to say, it was an easy decision to not recruit this athlete. Sometimes, the weeding out process doesn't take a great deal of thought, and if the athlete didn't even know what the SATs are, then he was certainly weeded out.

Don't Fall Asleep

I had the opportunity to recruit some very talented athletes while I was coaching at Syracuse. One that comes to mind when thinking about interesting recruiting stories is a high jumper I recruited one year that I really thought I had a legitimate chance of enrolling. This particular young man had high jumped 7'1" during the indoor season of his senior year in high school and coaches from all over the country were after him.

I made several phone calls to the student and his parents during the course of his senior year and then was invited to his home for a visit. The visit went very well, as I answered the family's questions and talked a great deal about the academic and athletic advantages for the young man if he attended our school. By the end of the evening, I was very confident that the student and his parents were very interested in the institution and I encouraged him to come up for an official overnight stay on our campus. He agreed to the idea and I went home very confident.

Several weeks later, I arranged for the student to come and stay overnight. He lived within a couple hours of our campus, so the family decided to drive so the father could also visit the school. We had some very talented athletes on our team at the time and several were also jumpers, so it was quite a simple decision as to who'd be the recruit's host. Everything was in place and the athlete arrived for his official visit.

He arrived on a Tuesday afternoon, attended practice, and then went out to dinner with members of the team. Our basketball team had a home game that night, so he and his host—along with 30,000 others—went up to the Carrier Dome after dinner and watched our basketball team chalk up another Big East victory. All had gone well the first night of his visit.

The following morning, his host took the recruit to class with him and then dropped him off at the admissions office for an interview and a tour of the campus. He met his dad in the admissions office and then I went and picked them up after the tour to have one final discussion with the dad, the athlete, and our head coach before they headed home.

We had a very nice lounge in our athletic facility that was designed for meetings with recruits, athletes on our team, and donors. Great historic pictures of Syracuse athletics on the walls, nice furniture, and even a big screen TV and a pool table. It was a great room to try to seal the deal. I brought the recruit and his dad into the room and our head coach was already seated and waiting for us. After the introductions, our head coach invited the recruit and his dad to sit down, as our coach was preparing to make the final pitch to ensure the student would attend Syracuse.

The recruit sat down on the couch, clad in ripped jeans, a torn sweatshirt, and a baseball hat. He proceeded to kick off his shoes, put his feet up on a coffee table, pull the hat over his eyes, and fall asleep. The dad did absolutely nothing to his son and listened contentedly as our coach continued with his brief sales pitch. When our head coach was done, the dad woke his son up and said: "Wake up. It's time for us to go home." We said our goodbyes and they departed for home.

The head coach and I went back to his office to discuss how the visit went. I told him everything had gone well other than the fact that the student had just fallen asleep and not paid attention to our head coach. In my opinion, he showed no respect for our program, our head coach, or me by doing that, so I mentioned this to the head coach. "Do we really want to have an athlete on our team for the next four years who thinks this is appropriate behavior?" We agreed—"No, we do not"—and I stopped recruiting the athlete on the spot.

About a month or so later, as the athletic scholarship signing date approached for our sport, the father gave me a call to inform me that several schools had offered his son a full scholarship and that they were still waiting for our offer. "Syracuse is my son's top choice," he informed me. "We're anxious for your offer so he can sign with you and we can get this whole process over with." I informed him we'd decided not to offer an athletic scholarship to his son and the dad immediately inquired as to why not. I told him that based on his actions in the meeting with our head coach that we'd decided we didn't think it was a sound investment to offer him a package.

The dad couldn't believe it. "You mean just because my son fell asleep during a stupid meeting with your head coach that you're not going to sign him?" Yes, I confirmed that this was an accurate understanding of the situation. The dad was dumbfounded as he clearly didn't think anything was wrong with his son falling asleep on our head coach, which clearly reconfirmed our decision in my opinion. To this day, I'm convinced we made the right decision in not signing this particular athlete, although I must admit it was a difficult pill to swallow when he went on to be a successful athlete at another school. You put in a great deal of effort out on the recruiting trail, and more often than not, it doesn't work out, but only once did it not work out due to falling asleep.

You're Transferring?

With some athletes you recruit, you know right from the start that either you're going to offer them a scholarship or they won't attend your school. With only 12.5 men's and 18 women's scholarships in track, a coach really does need to put a great deal of effort into recruiting quality athletes who you don't plan on offering any kind of athletic award to in order to fill out your roster with quality athletes.

I recruited a female high jumper one year who jumped 5'7" during her senior year of high school. We didn't intend on signing her to a scholarship but were very hopeful that she'd still enroll in our school, as she really would be able to help us in our conference championship. Many schools recruited her and she was certainly offered scholarships from at least a few colleges and universities, but thankfully, she decided to attend our school.

She came out for the team and had a great freshman year, scoring in the high jump in our indoor and outdoor conference championships. We were very satisfied with her success that year and told her at the end of the season we'd decided to offer her a partial scholarship for her sophomore year. I thought she'd have been ecstatic with the news that we were going to offer her an athletic scholarship for her last three years of college.

Instead, she stunned me with her response. "I'm transferring," she told me. "I'm leaving Syracuse at the end of the semester." When I asked her why, she informed me that she'd broken up with her boyfriend. "Your boyfriend?" I asked. "He doesn't even go to Syracuse. I thought he was a freshman at Colgate?" Mind you, Colgate and Syracuse are about 45 minutes apart. "Yes, he does go to Colgate," she responded. "The only reason I came to Syracuse in the first place is that it was the closest school to Colgate that I was accepted to. Now that we're no longer going out, there's no reason for me to stay here, so I'm transferring."

Talk about having your bubble burst. I'd spent the last year and a half thinking I'd done a fantastic job by recruiting this athlete to attend Syracuse even though other schools had offered her scholarships and come to find out I had nothing to do with it. Her entire decision was based on our school's proximity to where her boyfriend was going to school! To this day, whenever I get to the point where I think I'm doing a great job recruiting, I remind myself about this athlete and realize that 90 percent of the time— at the very least—the decisions that 17- and 18-year-old high school seniors make defy any kind of logic and we're fools to think we understand their thought process.

NCAA Basketball

Historically, the basketball team at Syracuse has been very good. For example, during my first year as a track coach there, the team included six athletes who eventually played in the NBA. During my seventh or eighth year there, the basketball team made it to the Final Four—the holy grail of college athletics. The entire city was in a frenzy and the student body was beside itself during the week leading up to the Final Four regional semifinals.

Several weeks prior to the basketball tournament even starting, I'd made a home visit in Virginia, as I was recruiting two outstanding senior athletes from the same high school. One of our other assistant coaches and I had flown down to Washington, DC, rented a car, and drove the half hour to one of the athlete's homes and had really done an outstanding job of selling the two seniors and their parents on our school. The girls were sold, and right there in the one young lady's living room, they agreed to fly up to Syracuse on a Monday several weeks later for an official visit.

I set the whole visit up, ordering plane tickets, arranging for hosts, ordering meal tickets, etc., for the two athletes to come up for a visit. It never occurred to me at the time I was setting up the visit that the night they were planning on staying overnight was the same night as the national championship in basketball nor did it occur to me that our men's basketball team would be playing in the game. But as luck would have it, the team stormed through the tournament and made it all the way to the championship game, where they were paired against the University of Kentucky.

I picked the two athletes up at the airport late in the morning on the day of the national championship and the first thing I did was explain to them that our basketball team was playing for the NCAA title that very night. They were aware of this fact and I was convinced these two kids were going to have the time of their lives spending the night on our campus, as the school was just riveted to the prospect of celebrating the team winning the national championship. I went on to tell the two of them as we drove the six or seven miles from the airport to the campus that they needed to understand that our practice that afternoon may be a little bit lethargic, as no one—and I mean no one—on our team, including the coaches, would be capable of focusing on practice that afternoon. Everyone on campus was so excited that I'm sure that if any professors gave exams on that particular Monday afternoon that the test scores would be worthless, as no one was able to concentrate on anything but the big game that night.

Needless to say, practice that afternoon revolved more around discussing the pending game and our beloved Orangemen's chances against Kentucky than track and field practice. Finally, about halfway through practice, the coaches decided to just send the kids back to their dorms, as it was quite apparent they weren't capable of a productive workout. The team and the two recruits departed the field house and went to the dining hall for dinner, certainly making plans as to where they were going to watch the game.

Kentucky ended up winning the game, and for the second time in about 10 years, Syracuse had to settle for runner-up in the national championship game in men's basketball. Second is still pretty darn good and the school received a great deal of free publicity over the three weeks of the tournament. I was still convinced that the two athletes were going to come to Syracuse. How could they not? They spent the evening on our campus during the greatest night in recent history at our school. I was positive that this experience alone would convince these two young ladies what a great place Syracuse was and what an athletic hotbed it was.

I picked them up in the morning in the dorms, took them back to the airport, and said goodbye. I told them I'd call soon and that I hoped they'd a good time on our campus. "Oh, yes," they responded. "It was very exciting to be here last night." I knew we had them.

A couple weeks later, we decided to offer both students an athletic scholarship and I called them to give them the good news. "Clearly," I thought, "these two are going to tell me they've decided to attend Syracuse." I called the first and offered her the scholarship and was totally dismayed at what she told me. "No, thank you, I've decided not to attend Syracuse. Your practices are far too unorganized." Unorganized? We were playing for the national championship that night. What did she expect? Undeterred, I called the second recruit, and amazingly enough, I was given the exact same rationale for turning down the offer. I was as frustrated as I'd ever been in recruiting. If an athlete can't understand how excited the kids on our team were for the pending basketball game, then what was I supposed to do? Sometimes, you can't know what a high school student is thinking.

You're Not Running?

Sometimes, even when they come to your school and after being recruited for an entire year, the kids decide not to come out for the team after they've enrolled. This can also be very frustrating, as you put in the effort for over a year, spend the summer really excited about the prospects of the upcoming season, and then discover when the school year begins that they never intended on running in the first place—they were just utilizing your assistance to ensure they're accepted to your school.

Every coach has heard the one where the athlete says he's decided not to compete his freshman year but would love to come out for the team his sophomore year after he gets settled in college. I've been coaching for almost 30 years and only once in my career has an athlete who told me that as a freshman ever ended up coming out for the team.

Then, you hear the justifiable reasoning: "I want to concentrate on my studies." No one will ever question that response, but I always make a mental note of the students who tell me they're having a difficult time adjusting to college and that they don't want to allow their grades to suffer, so they've decided not to compete. Inevitably, whenever I check the grades at the end of the semester, the kids who used that as their excuse for not running have higher than a 3.6 GPA.

Of course, kids will come up with a million reasons for not coming out for the team. "I'm joining the dance team," "I'm trying out for the orchestra," "I want to run for class vice president," and "I earned a spot in the fall play" are just a few of the excuses that coaches annually hear for why a recruit of theirs has decided not to come out for the team. Just once, I'd love to hear the honest response: "I just don't want to compete in college."

The most irrational response I've ever heard will haunt me for quite some time to come. I'd recruited a very good pole vaulter a few years ago and was excited when the young man decided to attend our school. He was really into track and loved being on the team. Shortly before finals his first semester, he had to have emergency surgery and had to delay taking his finals. He eventually finished all his exams and didn't do as well as he or his parents wanted.

Because he had the surgery, he was unable to compete during the indoor track season that winter and was unable to begin practicing with the team until mid-March—well into the second semester. When the freshman grade reports came, I was aware that he wasn't doing very well in school at all. I called him into my office and confronted him with the grade report. He responded: "Coach, I never wanted to go to college. My parents made me. I guess the only way I can prove to my parents that I don't want to go to college is to flunk all my classes and get kicked out."

I'd never heard that one before and admittedly had no immediate response. As hard as I tried the remainder of that spring to encourage him to go to class, I failed miserably in my attempt to convince him he'd been given a great opportunity and should take advantage of this gift. Sadly, he did indeed accomplish his objective and flunked out of college. His dad called me one day shortly after the grades came out and blamed the entire situation on track and field. "If my son hadn't been on the track team, this never would've happened," he rationalized.

Putting aside the fact he had emergency surgery at the end of the first semester and the fact that this surgery kept him away from practice for two-and-a-half months when everyone else on the team had been practicing and doing well in school, how was I supposed to respond to this statement? "By the way, sir, your son told me he had to prove to you he didn't want to go to college"? I couldn't say that, so I bit the bullet and allowed the kid's old man to blame the sport for his demise in school rather than pointing out the truth.

Recruiting is an inexact science—totally based on the decisions of 17- and 18-year-olds who have never even had to decide what to cook for dinner, let alone make a life-changing decision, such as the right college to choose for themselves. It's very, very difficult to have a career where, for good or bad, successes and failures are based entirely on whether young adults oftentimes not even old enough to vote decide whether they want to attend your institution.

6
Vans

iStockphoto/Thinkstock

Traveling with a large group of people can always be an interesting and complex endeavor. Add to that the diversity in size of a 130-pound distance runner versus a 260-pound shot-putter whose ages range from 18 to 22 and you'll always have the potential for disaster when you set foot on the road with a team of 65 athletes.

Travel for the intercollegiate track and field team can come in many different ways, shapes, and fashions—from a plane trip with an elite group of athletes to the other side of the country to the band-of-gypsies style of a bus, three vans, and a station wagon to a competition a few hours from campus. In my years involved in track and field, some of my more unusual and memorable travel stories have taken place in vans. Because of these strange but true experiences I've had traveling the countryside with my various track and field teams, I'd like to dedicate this chapter to Ford, General Motors, and Dodge for their ability to convince otherwise intelligent adults that you can fit 15 physically fit athletes and their luggage in a van.

Deer

My initial exposure to the trials and tribulations of van travel was actually my very first collegiate track meet—the first weekend in December during my freshman year. In retrospect, this experience was clearly an indication of things to come, and if I'd known that at the time, I'd have been better off ending my track career right then.

The Colgate track team practiced all fall my freshman year with great anticipation for our first indoor track meet of the season: the Syracuse Relays. Seemed a simple enough goal at the time, as Syracuse is only an hour drive from Colgate and what in the world could go wrong with a short drive like that? Back when I was a student at Colgate, our head coach was the only full-time track coach at the school and we had a roster of roughly 45 guys, but because we didn't travel by bus, transporting the entire team to away meets could be a rather complex task.

The school's solution to our travel dilemma was to allow upperclassmen on the team to take a van driving test, certify the students to drive, and then let students have the responsibility of driving the team to the away competitions. I'm sure this driving test wasn't very complicated, and over the years, it became quite apparent to me that there were people driving these vans on trips that had no business driving a van across a parking lot, let alone across state lines. I remember on one such trip in rather inclement weather that the upperclassman chauffer was driving way too fast for the conditions, and when one of our teammates suggested he slow down, as we were hydroplaning, the driver's response was: "What difference does it make how fast I'm driving? We'll be hydroplaning whether I'm going 10 miles per hour or 60 miles per hour and I have a date tonight, so we might as well go 60."

Anyway, getting back to the Syracuse Relays. The meet was scheduled to be an all-day affair—beginning at 10 a.m. and concluding well after dinnertime. Falling on the first weekend in December, the meet was immediately prior to finals at Colgate and probably at all the other schools competing in the meet. Because it was right before finals, our coach decided that when enough athletes were done competing to fill up a van, he'd send a group of us back to school with a student driver in order to study. The drive from Syracuse to Hamilton may only be an hour, but Route 20—the road one takes between the two communities—isn't exactly an interstate, as it's hilly, dark, and only one lane in each direction for extended stretches.

As luck would have it and as is the case with most December days in central New York, it was snowing on our way home. As we departed Manley Field House, it seemed like a rather simple trip, but as we continued on, the weather began to deteriorate quite rapidly. As a freshman, I was relegated to the backseat, which means if you put 15 people in a van, four people are in the backseat. As we were driving down a hill about 20 minutes from home, I saw a herd of deer running through a field, heading directly for the road in front of us. Before I could finish frantically screaming "Look out for the deer," we hit a deer head-on in the front of the van. Within 10 seconds, the front of the van looked like Old Faithful, as the radiator had broken and fluid was shooting straight up in the air.

Of course, being a Saturday night and only 20 minutes from home, the immediate consensus in the van was to carry on—radiator or no radiator. That argument lasted no longer than a minute, though, as the van shuttered to a deathly silence in the middle of the road a matter of moments after hitting the deer. Fortunately for us, a farmhouse was directly across the road from where we'd stopped and we all trudged through the snow to its front door. The only one home was a 16-year-old guy who came to the door wearing a flannel jacket with his New York State hunting license pinned to the back of his jacket.

When we explained our predicament, he leaped with excitement—much to the surprise of a van load of kids who all had grown up in metropolitan New York. Before we realized what he was up to, he was out the front door and across the highway to where we'd told him the deer had been struck. While he was out on the highway, the driver of our van called back to campus to have someone come pick us up and was told that in order to fill out the proper insurance information for the school, he'd have to call the state police.

A state trooper arrived a few minutes later and asked us if we wanted the deer because in New York, only the driver of the car that hit the deer can claim the carcass. When he was told we didn't want the deer, the state trooper went across the highway to look for the deer in order to tag it and have the state come pick it up. To his surprise, he found the spot where the deer had been hit and also where it had come to its final resting place, but the deer was no longer there. The state cop took down our driver's statement, gave him the necessary paperwork for the insurance, and then departed. After the state trooper left, we all went out back to the barn of the farmhouse in search of our young host, and low and behold, he had the deer in the barn—already gutted—and had the hide hanging from the ceiling of the barn and the guts spread out all over the floor of the barn.

Minutes later, a university official arrived with another van and we all packed up and headed home. As we were departing the farmhouse, our 16-year-old host couldn't thank us enough for hitting the deer in front of his house, as he told us he'd now be able to go to school the following Monday and let all his friends know he had indeed bagged a deer during the 1979 hunting season. To this day, when I drive from Syracuse to Hamilton across Route 20, I always slow down when I pass that farmhouse and get a chuckle as to how excited that young man was at our misfortune that cold December night so many years ago.

Before I go on, I think it's imperative to describe to those of you who have never been in a van how the manufacturers intend for a group to fit 15 people into one of these motorized disasters waiting to happen. The front seats are just an individual seat for the driver and one for the front passenger. Behind the front seat are four rows of seats. The first three are designed for three people, although not three large adults, and then the last row is supposed to seat four comfortably, although four in the fifth row of a van and comfortable aren't synonymous words in my vocabulary. Needless to say, it's very, very difficult to put 15 adult males into a 15-passenger van.

Ten Hours in the Backseat

During late March of my freshman year, we went on our annual spring trip, with 43 athletes, two coaches, two vans driven by the coaches, and one van driven by a senior athlete. Naturally, the freshmen were immediately relegated to the back rows of each of the three vans, and when you throw in a week's worth of luggage as well as all the track and field equipment, only one word comes to mind: claustrophobic.

Our journey began Friday afternoon immediately after we all had completed a week of midterm exams—destined for the Towson State Relays on Saturday in Towson, Maryland. Everyone was excited in anticipation of a week away from campus and the opportunity to compete in a climate warmer than central New York in early spring, so the first leg of our trip—roughly six hours—went by quickly and smoothly.

We successfully competed at Towson State on Saturday, and despite the constant rain throughout the entire meet, my teammates and I were all still quite upbeat about the week away from campus that lay ahead, as we'd left upstate New York in late March heading south and anything—even an all-day track meet in the rain—was better than what the weather had been like in Hamilton since mid-November: snowy and cold. After the meet, we packed up the vans—now not only with 43 athletes, two coaches, and a week's worth of luggage and track and field equipment but also an entire day's worth of wet, soggy, smelly track uniforms with a new destination: George Mason University in Fairfax, Virginia, a suburb of Washington, DC.

We practiced at George Mason from Sunday through Thursday, sleeping four to a room in a motel that didn't remotely resemble a five-star hotel. By this time, many of the guys' spirits began to sour a little as they started to realize their college roommates and fraternity brothers were basking in the sun in Florida or Bermuda with a beer in one hand and heaven only knows what in the other hand while we were practicing twice a day in cold and rainy conditions, so we weren't even getting a little tan. We did survive our week in Fairfax though, and on Thursday, we set out on the last leg of our journey, traveling from Fairfax to Williamsburg for the College of William & Mary and the Colonial Relays.

Nothing is more satisfying to an athlete than practicing hard for a given period of time and then being rewarded for the hard work with a great competition. To succeed in outdoor track, though, the weather must cooperate. When we'd left Hamilton in the snow and cold, most of us had packed sunglasses and suntan oil (there wasn't a hole in the ozone layer yet), as we'd inaccurately assumed that because we were heading south that we were heading into warm weather. The weather in Virginia in late March and early April may be nicer than upstate New York, but no one can guarantee it will be tropical at that time of the year. Sadly for us, the weather gods decided to make the first weekend in April that year quite cold in Virginia.

So, we competed all day Friday and Saturday in rather inclement weather, and after a week on the road—during which we'd initially driven six hours south and then three more hours south and then finally another hour south—we found ourselves 10 hours from home. The meet concluded at 6 p.m. Saturday and our coach was suddenly in a big hurry to get home. As if our taking an extra 20 minutes to shower and change was going to slow our arrival home by several hours? So, at 6 p.m. on Saturday night as the meet ended and we were still dressed in our track uniforms—all the way down to wet socks and jockstraps—we all packed into the three vans, with the 43 athletes, two coaches, the track equipment, and nine days' worth of wet, dirty laundry that had started out the week as our luggage and off for home we went.

I tell this story to give you a better idea as to what true van travel is all about, sitting in the middle of the back seat of a 15-passenger van in soaking wet clothes with gear that's now growing green with algae and traveling 10 hours in the pitch black with 40 other people who a week earlier were really excited about traveling together and now want nothing more than to get back to class and away from each other. The only pleasant memory of the entire ride home was that it happened to be Easter weekend, and as we finally pulled back into Hamilton as the sun was rising on Easter morning, I saw a rabbit cross the road, and to this day, I honestly think I saw the rabbit carrying jelly beans. Maybe not, but you'd be surprised what kind of tricks the mind can play on you after breathing wet jockstraps for 10 hours in the back of a van.

Gas? Who Needs Gas?

When I was in school, we frequently competed at the University of Rochester. Colgate and Rochester are schools with similar academic reputations, roughly the same size, and only two-and-a-half hours apart. One February Friday night, we had a meet at Rochester, and as was the case my freshman year with the meet at Syracuse, a van was sent home as soon as enough guys were done competing to fill it up.

This particular night, I happened to be one of the last to compete, so I was in one of the last two vans to depart for home—and boy did I picked the wrong van. The other van was driven by the coach and he told us he'd meet us at the McDonald's by the entrance to the New York State Thruway. Yes, McDonald's. Perhaps no track team in America doesn't select speed over quality in dining selections when in a hurry. On this particular night, quality nutrition wasn't a priority, as Friday night meant fraternity parties at Colgate and a rare Saturday without a meet meant a reason to party.

When we arrived at McDonald's, it was already closed (this was the era before 24-hour-a-day fast food) and our coach and his van departed McDonald's for the highway before we arrived at the fast-food restaurant. Our driver—some acne-faced 21-year-old—informed us as we were pulling out of the McDonald's parking lot that we needed to find an open gas station before we started for home because the van was almost on empty. We were unable to find an open service station, so we eventually surmised that we could certainly make it to the first rest stop on the thruway before running out of gas. We got on the highway and bets were already being taken from the back of the van as to whether we'd make it to the rest stop on the little gas remaining in the tank. We eventually got to the point where the signs on the side of the highway were advertising for the rest stop—only two miles away—which was met by hoots and hollers of relief from all inside the van. As fate would have it, we ran out of gas exactly one mile from the rest stop as the van came to a stop directly next to the "One mile to rest stop" sign.

This didn't appear to be a problem because we're a track team and we're in great shape! Except the van was loaded with throwers and jumpers—none of whom could walk a mile if our lives depended on it and certainly not just for gas. We had one distance runner in the van, but only an hour before, he had run a three-mile race and had tossed his cookies on the finish line judge at the end of his race, so he was in no shape to run a mile down a dark highway in the middle of the winter. Cooler heads—or, at the very least, bigger people—prevailed and this poor, undernourished distance runner was told by a senior thrower weighing 250 pounds not to debate this issue. "I don't care if you threw up an hour ago," the thrower said. "You're a distance runner. You go get the gas."

So, out he went into the cold and ran the mile up to the rest stop, bought a gas can and a couple gallons of fuel, ran back, emptied the contents of his purchase into the van, and up to the rest stop we went to fill up the tank. No democracy on a track team—the big guys order the little guys around. We made it back a little late that night to the fraternity parties and I'm sure to this day that poor skinny distance runner still harbors resentment toward big guys.

Lake Champlain

I'm not sure about the validity of this story, but during my freshman year, I heard this story so many times that it became my reality whether it actually happened or not. The story took place the year before I arrived at Colgate and is so unbelievable that even though I wasn't directly involved, I had to include this tale, as all the upperclassmen on our team swore it was true.

Apparently, during my senior year of high school, Colgate had an indoor track meet at the University of Vermont. UVM is in Burlington, Vermont, which sits right on the eastern shore of Lake Champlain. Lake Champlain is the border between New York and Vermont in northeastern New York State. The folklore of this story is that the drivers of the Colgate vans missed the exit off the New York State Thruway, which would've taken them south of Lake Champlain and north of Lake George in order to get from eastern New York into southern Vermont.

Supposedly, by the time the drivers finally realized their error, they were well north of the southern tip of Lake Champlain. They exited the thruway and stopped at a gas station and asked the attendant for directions to head back south to go around the lake. The gas station attendant scoffed at their request as to how to backtrack an hour or so south to get back to their initial route around the south side of the lake and he pointed out that the lights on the other side of the lake from his service station were indeed from the town of Burlington. The attendant stated that he'd been ice fishing that very morning over on the Vermont side of the lake and surely if his pickup truck had no problems maneuvering on the lake that the vans could too.

Not a very tough decision for any clear-thinking, mature adult, you'd think. It may take an additional hour to go south around the lake and back north on the other side, but at least safety would be assured for all, so that's what should have been done, right? Wrong. We're talking about a track team full of seasoned veterans of van adventures. "Go across the lake," the track team members screamed in unison. "We'll make it!" I wasn't on the trip and have always been a bit skeptical about this story, but every upperclassman on the team my freshman year swore that indeed the team drove across the lake on a plowed section of Lake Champlain to get to the University of Vermont. Believe it or not, it's certainly a story worthy of gray hairs for any parent of a collegiate athlete.

The remainder of my own college career was rather uneventful as far as van rides go, but once I started coaching, the strange but true van adventures began to multiply at an unfortunately rapid rate.

Snow Shovels

My first year as an assistant coach at Colgate was more of a learning experience as a grunt rather than actually coaching any specific athletes. I was relegated to a plethora of menial tasks that our head coach didn't have enough time to do. In late March, I was finally given some real responsibility, as I was asked to take Tim, our top decathlete, to the University of Virginia so he could compete in a warm weather decathlon while the rest of the team stayed north and competed at Cornell University.

As with many of the stories I have from my days at Colgate and Syracuse, snow is an intricate aspect of the tale. Tim and I left Hamilton on a mild Thursday morning with a rather straightforward eight-hour drive in front of us. Normally, if the weather was cooperating when we left Hamilton and driving south, we were home free, although this wouldn't end up being a normal day, as the weather was great in upstate New York and, unbeknownst to us, a storm was well to our south and in our direct path.

A decathlon is a series of 10 events over two days. The first day begins with the 100 meters and is then followed in succession by the long jump, shot put, and high jump and concludes with the 400 meters. The second day begins with the 110-meter high hurdles, continues with the discus, pole vault, and javelin, and finishes with the 1,500 meters. The average pole vault pole is anywhere from 14 to 16 feet in length and a javelin is more than 6 feet long. When traveling by car or van, coaches and athletes have devised a variety of creative ways to tie the poles and javelins to the outside of the vehicle. We started off on our trip with three poles and two javelins tied to the outside of the car and several discuses and shot puts in the trunk, along with three days' worth of luggage.

The first two hours of our trip from Hamilton to Scranton, Pennsylvania, went smoothly, but by the time we'd made it to Scranton, it had started to snow, although nothing significant. The drive between Scranton and Harrisburg, Pennsylvania, normally takes about two hours, with almost nothing of interest to see along the route and very few exits. The snow that day between Scranton and Harrisburg began to come down rather heavily and traffic was limited to the right-hand lane despite the fact we were on an interstate. Between Scranton and Harrisburg, the route travels straight through the Pocono Mountains and part of the Appalachian Trail, and as we traveled through the Poconos, traffic was nearly at a standstill in some places and there were times when we were traveling for more than an hour at speeds between 10 and 15 miles per hour.

Tim and I continued to discuss our options, but every time we thought it was time to give up and turn around and go home, we'd hit a clear spot, the traffic would pick up its pace, and we'd conclude that the worst was over and that we should continue. By the time we'd traveled to Harrisburg, we were at least four-and-a-half hours behind schedule and we knew we had no chance of making it all the way to Charlottesville,

Virginia, that day, so we decided to continue until dinner and then find a hotel for the night and drive the rest of the way to Virginia in the morning—the day of the decathlon.

Shortly after Harrisburg, the snow stopped and a light drizzle replaced the white stuff, so we drove another hour and stopped in Chambersburg, Pennsylvania, just north of the Maryland border. We had dinner and checked into a hotel, and as the rain continued to fall, we went to sleep, knowing we'd have to get up early in order to reach Charlottesville by noon for the 1 p.m. starting time of the decathlon.

When I awoke in the morning, I couldn't believe my eyes, as what had been rain the night before had turned into a serious blizzard during the course of the night. From the hotel's parking lot, I could see the highway and there was absolutely no traffic moving on the interstate. Not only was our van entirely covered with snow, but the hotel parking lot was too, as I soon discovered that the hotel didn't have a contract with a snow removal company for their lot. Many others were also in the parking lot with the same predicament we were in: late for something and having stopped at this hotel the night before to get out of the poor weather with the objective of starting out anew in the morning. But none of us were going anywhere, as we were stuck in a parking lot, and even if we were capable of getting out, the interstate was impassable too.

After surveying the parking lot and determining that Tim and I were at least temporarily stuck in the hotel, I went to the front desk and inquired as to the length of time expected for the clearing of the hotel's parking lot and of the highway's status. Before I could even get the questions out of my mouth, I was asked by the front desk clerk, "Are you a guest of the hotel?" When I told him yes, his response was quick and shocking: "Don't forget checkout is 10 a.m. If you stay in your room past 10, I'll have to charge you for an additional night." When I asked him how he expected me to check out of his hotel when I couldn't get out of his parking lot, he shrugged his shoulders and said, "Sorry, sir, but hotel policy states that checkout is at 10 a.m. and that if you're in your room after 10, you'll be charged an additional night's fee."

I called the track office at the University of Virginia and discovered that we weren't the only ones stuck hours away due to the weather and therefore the start of the meet had been delayed a day. So, Tim and I decided we wouldn't turn around and head home but rather continue on to UVA.

By 10 a.m., the parking lot still wasn't cleared, but Route 81 was now passable. Several hotel guests had walked across the street to a hardware store and purchased snow shovels, but the hotel's parking lot was insurmountable for mere shovels. At 10:15, as we continued to attempt to shovel our way out of the parking lot, the hotel manager came out and incredibly demanded that either we vacate the premises or pay for an additional night's stay. Despite my better judgment, I went into the hotel lobby, paid the man for another night—for fear that if we couldn't get out that we'd have nowhere to stay—and returned outside and continued to shovel.

As if on cue, within 15 minutes of the hotel's guests paying for an additional night, a snowplow arrived and plowed the hotel's parking lot clean as a whistle. Along with the other suckers who'd paid, I went into the lobby and asked for my money back and, of course, the manager refused.

Tim and I packed up the car and headed out of a hotel I'd never endorse to my worst enemy. Fortunately, the weekend wasn't a total waste, as by the time we reached Virginia, the weather had turned into a pleasant spring weekend and Tim accomplished what we'd gone down there to do: qualify for the IC4A men's Division I Easterns. The trip home the day after the meet was a placid spring day, and as we entered Pennsylvania, Tim jokingly suggested we stop in Chambersburg for a bite to eat and to stop by our favorite hotel just to see if they'd like to take more of our money for no apparent reason. Of course, we didn't stop.

Since then, I've coached a couple athletes from Chambersburg and I've always told them that story. The last time I told the story, though, I was informed by the athlete that the hotel in question had gone out of business and the building had been torn down. Surprise, surprise—justice was served. Better late than never is what I always say.

Sleeping in Vans

My first year at Syracuse, we took a group of athletes to the Yale Invitational in early January. We had 16 people on the trip, so we took a van and a car. One of our other assistants drove the car and I drove the van with 12 people in it—a little bit more room than my days at Colgate but still a pretty crowded van. Our team was loaded that year with great throwers, one of whom would later go on to win several U.S. national titles in the discus, place fourth in two separate Olympic Games, and win a World Championships title in the discus before he retired and another athlete was an All-American in the hammer throw. So, even though we only had 12 people in the van, it was still quite crowded for a five-hour drive because the majority of the occupants were elite throwers and all rather large young men.

We made it to New Haven very easily, and as a team, we were quite successful. The meet gave out very nice watches to the winners in each event, and if I recall correctly, we brought home more than our fair share of Yale Invitational timepieces. Most indoor meets end around 6 p.m. and the meet in New Haven was no exception, so as soon as the meet ended, the kids showered and we loaded up the van for the five-hour ride home, expecting to arrive home before midnight After stopping to eat somewhere within the first hour of the trip, the kids all fell asleep and I was left on my own to contemplate the meaning of life and the dark blank road in front of me, as the car with other members of our team trailed directly behind me.

When we arrived in Middletown, New York, which was about the halfway point, we left Route 84 and headed north on Route 17. Route 17 is a dark road with moderate traffic, traversing through small towns and the Catskill Mountains. The only reason anyone outside of central New York would at all be familiar with this stretch of modest highway is it happens to be the road that 300,000 young adults exited to get to Bethel, New York, home of the 1969 Woodstock Music & Art Fair.

Somewhere north of Middletown, it started to rain, which in mid-January in central New York is rather unusual, as it's normally too cold to rain. Maybe I was tired or maybe I just wasn't experienced enough driving in weather like that, but somewhere along the way, the rain stopped being plain old rain and turned into a very icy, messy, dangerous sleet/rain. I continued to drive the speed limit because I didn't realize that the road had begun to freeze underneath our tires, as there was little if any traffic in our direction, so I had nothing to gauge our speed in relationship to the weather conditions.

At one point, though, we came upon a police car in front of us driving in the right-hand lane. With no exits or off-ramps in sight, I was a tad confused when we approached the slow-moving police car in the right-hand lane, as he had turned his right-hand blinker on as we drew nearer. I mistook the right blinker as an indication that he was pulling over and that he wanted me to go around him. I pulled out into the left-hand lane, and as soon as I passed the police car, I lost total control of the van and took the van into a 360-degree spin directly to the left of the cop car. Miraculously, as the van came to a stop, we were facing in the correct direction in the left-hand shoulder of the road and somehow had come out of the 360 intact and without hitting the cop.

The cop got out of his car and slowly lumbered over to the driver's side window of our van and said, "What the hell were you thinking about?" When I responded with "You turned your right-hand blinker on, so I thought you were pulling off the road and you wanted me to pass you," he almost fell over in amazement that I'd think to pass him on such an icy night. But I guess he couldn't argue with my logic or, more realistically, he was affected by the sight of 12 sets of wide-opened, frightened, and stunned sets of eyes, because he let me off with the warning that indeed the road was dangerous and that we needed to be more cautious the remainder of our trip. He clearly didn't have to warn me twice, as my entire body was shaking and I was a little surprised that I hadn't soiled myself.

We were able to get off the shoulder rather easily with all the weight we had in the van, and about 20 minutes later—only 15 minutes south of Binghamton and our return to a major highway—I came around a corner at the bottom of a long steep hill and thought I'd just ended up on the Las Vegas strip.

Lights were everywhere—police cars, tow trucks, headlights, taillights—as the entire area was lit up like the Fourth of July. I made it halfway up the hill when I realized that the reason for all the lights was that the road was too steep to ascend with all the ice on the road. I was halfway up the hill in the left-hand lane with cars stuck in front of me and to the right of me and cars speeding up behind me and I was unable to continue to move forward. I put the van in park, had my foot on the brake, and also put the emergency brake on. My right foot was shaking as it rested on the brake, as I was so nervous. At one point shortly after stopping, the driver of the car behind me knocked on my window and said: "Tell the girl in the backseat of your van to stop combing her hair. Every time she strokes her hair, your van is sliding to the right across the road." Despite the athlete discontinuing her beauty session, within 10 minutes of our initial stop, our van had slid from the middle of the left-hand lane all the way across the road and rested to a stop in the right-hand shoulder.

The guys on the team had to get out of the van and push us to ensure we squeezed onto the shoulder between two cars that were already stuck there. One of the guys was so utterly disgusted with our predicament that he opened our medical kit, pulled out a bottle of cough syrup, and chugged the entire bottle, saying as he did it: "If we're spending the night in the van, then I'm going to pass out and sleep through this hell." Sure enough, he fell asleep, and eventually, we did too.

A couple hours later, I woke up and was surprised to see that there were no longer any other cars stuck on the road. We slept right through the sanders coming through and making the road passable. We slept through all the other cars starting their engines and leaving the area behind. We slept through everything until the exact same cop to whom I'd proven my masterful driving skills hours before again knocked on our window and this time asked, "What the hell are you doing here?" This time, my story seemed even less possible than the first time, but he went back to his car to radio in to verify that indeed this road had been impassable a few hours earlier. He returned to the van and pleaded with me to drive safely the rest of the way home and begged me not to give him a chance to run into him again that night.

We didn't and he didn't and we finally made it home. Our discus-throwing, cough syrup–chugging passenger actually had a serious hangover when we got back to Syracuse, so I guess the moral of this story is don't drink too much cough syrup because it can give you a whale of a headache. By the way, keeping in mind our estimate of arriving home at midnight, we pulled into the field house parking lot back in Syracuse at 7:30 a.m.

Last-Chance Qualifier

Although the qualifying procedures for the NCAA Division I Outdoor Championship have changed since I left coaching at that level, when I was coaching in Division I, the NCAA track rules committee would establish a set of qualifying standards each year. If you met the qualifying standard in any meet during the season, you qualified for the NCAA Championship. There also were established dates that created the parameters from a scheduling standpoint as to when the qualifying could take place. The week leading up to the last potential day for qualifying oftentimes became a nightmare, as teams would be chasing the standard at various last-chance qualifier meets all over the country. When this story took place, the last day to qualify was on a Thursday.

We'd returned from the IC4A Championship late the previous Sunday night after an eight-hour bus drive from James Madison University in Harrisonburg, Virginia. Why we didn't just stay down in that neck of the woods is beyond me, but it sure created a great deal of traveling the following week. Georgetown University was hosting a last-chance meet on Wednesday night, so on Tuesday morning, we packed up a vanload of athletes who'd only been home for 48 hours and drove right back down to within an hour of where we'd been just two days prior.

The meet on Wednesday night ended at 9 p.m. and didn't go as well as we would've liked from a performance standpoint, as none in our van improved on their seasonal-best performances. We asked around as to where the closest meet was on Thursday—the last day to qualify. "The University of North Carolina is having a meet tomorrow afternoon," we were told. So, without a second thought, we packed up the van and left Washington, DC, at 9:30 p.m. and drove the several hours south to Chapel Hill.

Arriving in Chapel Hill at about 3 a.m., we found a hotel with vacancies and checked in, telling the kids that the meet started the next day at noon, so we'd be checking out of the hotel at 10:30 a.m. and that they'd better get some sleep. We checked out in the morning and arrived at the track by 11—only to discover an empty track. After finding someone in the track office, we were informed that the meet had been changed to 5 p.m. "Didn't you receive the fax we sent out yesterday afternoon?" Well, no, of course we hadn't received it. We were in Washington, DC, yesterday afternoon and no one at the meet had deemed it important to inform us of the change in start time.

Once again, we packed up the van and found a hotel that was willing to rent us some rooms for a few hours and the kids got a few more hours of sleep. I must admit that historically, when we went on these wild goose chases for qualifying standards, it normally didn't work out. But this meet was a great success for our team, as of the seven athletes we had with us, four of them ended up meeting the standard in their respective event that night and made it into the NCAA Championship. Mission accomplished! At the conclusion of the meet around 9 p.m., our only objective was to get the van packed and start heading north. Did we accomplish that goal? Yes. Was it the last thing to go right that night? You bet!

I don't remember the route number of the highway that connects Chapel Hill to Richmond, but what I do remember is that I had never before nor have I ever since then seen a road blessed with more tall overhanging evergreens in my life. Pretty in the day time, I'm sure, but extremely dark at night, which is rather unfortunate when you're not sure where you're going and are very tired. We continued to make progress, and as the majority of the passengers slept, I was beginning to believe it was realistic to think that we could make it all the way home that night, although I didn't share my optimism with anyone else, as I knew this ridiculous idea would've been construed as potential suicide.

Somewhere along the way, one of the passengers woke up and asked me if it were foggy outside. I said, "No, why do you ask?" and was greeted with a response that

I hadn't noticed myself. "The windshield is awfully fogged up, don't you think?" As the student asked the question, I glanced down at the thermostat and realized that the van was overheating, so I pulled over to the side of the highway to assess the situation.

What was our situation? Midnight, somewhere in northern North Carolina or southern Virginia, on a dark highway with little if any traffic, no food, no water, no way to communicate for help (this is before cell phones), and a van full of African American athletes—all of whom were convinced they couldn't get out of the van for fear that the Ku Klux Klan was about to emerge from the woods and take us all captive. About a half hour after we pulled over, a state trooper came by, who I think had watched too many Andy Griffith reruns, as his speech, body language, and general attitude exactly resembled Barney Fife. He did call for help, though, and within another half hour, a tow truck came alongside us with a driver who'd clearly been asleep for several hours when our police friend had called and requested his help on our behalf.

As our savior emerged from the truck, leaving his German Shepherd inside the cab of his truck, he released a cupful of tobacco juice from his mouth that would've made Clint Eastwood or a big league baseball player proud. He rambled over to our van and smiled a big toothless grin and in a classic southern accent asked, "What seems to be the problem, y'all?" After assessing the situation, he informed us it was against Virginia state law to tow a vehicle with people in it but that we wouldn't all fit in his pickup truck. His solution? "Hell, it's late. No one's gonna know I towed your van with y'all in it if y'all don't tell and I sure as hell ain't going to tell no one, so let's go." So, off we went down the highway—eight of us in a van being towed by a toothless, tired, German Shepherd–owning mechanic. But, hey, at least we finally knew we'd made it to Virginia.

We got off the highway and for what seemed like an eternity, although afterward we discovered was four miles, traveled up some backcountry roads and finally arrived at his garage/trailer park/fishing hole/convenience store. Upon arrival at his place of business, he invited everyone out of the van, although with several dogs running around and with the majority of the inhabitants of the van still convinced that a sighting of the Ku Klux Klan was might be inevitable, we all chose to stay in the van and feed the dogs chocolate chip cookies through the cracks in the open van windows. Our savior finally found the problem—a ruptured water hose, which he thankfully had in stock.

Within a matter of minutes, he'd replaced the hose and refilled the radiator and we were as good as new. When Andy, the other assistant track coach on the trip with me, asked the mechanic "How much do we owe you?" I was convinced that the response was going to be "Well, boy, how much you got?" But my faith in humanity south of the Mason-Dixon line was restored that night as this poor man who'd been awakened out of bed at 1 a.m., towed us at least 15 miles, and then fixed our van responded with an astonishing "$39.95."

One of the athletes on that van ride was Qadry Ismail. Qadry's brother, Rahib Ismail, had been runner-up in the Heisman Trophy voting the previous fall as a wide receiver at the University of Notre Dame. Qadry was also an All-American football player and would go on to play many years as a wide receiver in the NFL, including starting for the Baltimore Ravens the year they won the Super Bowl in 2000. The entire night the mechanic kept on looking into our van in a manner that the kids all perceived as menacing, but after our mechanic finally fixed the van, he sheepishly said to us as we were getting ready to leave, "Is that the Missile?" which was Qadry's nickname. When we confirmed that it was the Missile, he responded very quietly, "Can I have your autograph?"

Anyone who watched Qadry when he was an NFL analyst for ESPN knows he has a really, loud, pleasing, and infectious laugh. I never heard Qadry laugh any louder than he did that night as he signed the mechanic's autograph and his stress and fear were released with that one innocent request for an autograph.

Once again, we packed up and headed back down the road with a huge sigh of relief, and within a few minutes, my passengers were fast asleep. A little after dawn, when we were well north of Washington, DC, Andy woke up and I'm sure saw a set of white knuckles glued to the steering wheel. Despite my repeated and confident insistence that I was fine and that I could indeed make it all the way home without stopping, wiser heads prevailed and Andy made me pull off and find a hotel so everyone could sleep in a bed for a few hours. I'm sure I fell asleep within seconds of hitting the pillow in my room.

We finally made it home on Friday afternoon—able to unpack for a couple days, feeling tired and worn out but also happy with the success of the meet. On Monday, we packed up again and got into a van—but this time only to drive up to the Syracuse airport to fly to Eugene, Oregon, and the NCAA Championship. A bigger group than we would've had if we hadn't driven to Chapel Hill, so it was all worth it. When the season ended a couple weeks later, we asked our equipment manager for one of Qadry's old football jerseys and sent it as a final thank you to our friendly mechanic in southern Virginia.

A Bear

One of the greatest decisions college administrators have made in my coaching career is the recognition that vans are dangerous. I'm quite certain that the stories I've told so far are the norm for all college coaches, not the exception. Too many negative situations—many with far worse outcomes than the ones I've described—finally led administrators to realize that the few dollars saved by having teams travel by vans instead of by bus aren't worth the potentially devastating risks. By the time I began coaching at Muhlenberg, van travel had basically become obsolete, although I have one particularly interesting van story from my days here in Allentown.

In Division I, the men's eastern championship is referred to as the IC4As. At the Division III level, the equivalent meet is the Eastern College Athletic Conference (ECAC) Championship. Several years ago, the outdoor ECAC Championship was held at

Williams College, in Williamstown, Massachusetts. A beautiful, small New England town, Williamston sits in the northwestern corner of Massachusetts, with Vermont directly to the north and New York directly to the west. The town and the college epitomize small town New England and offer a wonderful setting for a track meet.

The meet is always held on the third Thursday and Friday of May, which happens to coincide with Muhlenberg College's senior week, concluding with Sunday's graduation. We left Williamstown at around 7 p.m. on Friday, with the seniors on the trip pleading with me not to stop for dinner or for any other reason, as they urged me to get back them back to campus as soon as possible so they could celebrate with their classmates. I did the best I could to accommodate the seniors' request and made it almost the entire trip home without having to make a stop.

Around 11 p.m. and only 45 minutes from home, I could no longer hold my bladder, as I'd probably drank far too much caffeine that afternoon. We were driving in western New Jersey on Route 78 when I saw a sign for a rest stop. Not realizing that this particular rest stop didn't have comfort facilities but rather was only a parking rest stop, I pulled the van off the highway to relieve myself.

I should have recognized immediately that something was a tad unusual, as here it was a Friday night at 11 on an interstate and the parking lot was filled with cars. Not only did that not tip me off to the fact that something was awry, but the fact that all the cars had people sitting in them wide awake also didn't register with me. I got out of the van, leaving all the kids sleeping inside, and strolled over to a tree far away from all the cars. Not a single person in any of the other vehicles said anything to me as I walked over to my chosen tree, and as I unzipped by pants and as I started to relieve myself, I noticed that the tree I was standing under was shaking. I looked up and all the sudden saw a rather large animal in the tree. I zipped my pants back up and started to walk back to the van, and as I did so, an adult black bear hopped down from the tree and started to rumble after me toward our van. As I was cautiously yet hurriedly making my way back to the van, I noticed a great deal of smiling and laughing by the people in the parked cars.

When I safely got back to the van with the doors locked, I awoke the entire van to point out the bear that was now only a couple feet away from our van, as there was no way anyone would've believed me if I'd allowed them to continue to sleep. What was initially anger at my waking them up quickly turned to astonishment and fear and then outright excitement as the team watched the bear knock over a trash can sitting a few feet away from us. We must have stayed for 15 or 20 minutes, entertained by the animal as all desire to return for senior night activities was briefly forgotten.

I still don't know why all those cars were in the parking lot, but the only conclusion I've been able to come to is that local people in that area of New Jersey must have known that a bear frequents that rest stop and they park their cars to watch the bear. I only wish that if that were the case, someone should have had the decency to inform me of my impending doom as I walked right up to and under the tree that the bear happened to be sitting in. Only in New Jersey!

He Forgot to Change His Clock

When I was at Syracuse, we almost always went to an invitational at the University of Miami the first weekend in April. This was quite a few years ago and prior to the energy bill that President George W. Bush passed that included an increase in the number of weeks of daylight savings time. Back before the bill, clocks were changed the last weekend in October and the first weekend in April rather than the first weekend of November and the third weekend in March, as we do now.

Whenever we competed at the University of Miami, we always stayed in a hotel right across the street from the campus, which was quite convenient, as we all could walk from the hotel to the track. Because the hotel was within walking distance of the track, we only had to hire a bus company to pick us up from the airport on Thursday afternoon and drop us off at the hotel and then come back and pick us up at the hotel on Sunday morning in order to take us back to the airport rather than hiring a bus for the entire time we were in Miami.

On Saturday night after the meet was over and when we'd returned to the hotel from dinner, the coaches called for a team meeting to discuss the meet and go over our departure plans for the following morning. We repeated over and over again to the kids that they needed to remember to change their clocks before they went to bed and to make sure they also arranged a wakeup call with the hotel operator. We absolutely covered all our bases regarding the time change—or so we thought.

Sunday morning arrived. I got up, showered, and went down to the lobby of the hotel, and within 10 minutes, every coach and every athlete in our travel party were in the lobby—with bags packed and room keys returned—and we were ready to go. Then, we waited and waited and waited. Guess who forgot to change his clock? The bus driver scheduled to take us to the airport. The bus company we'd contracted wasn't from Miami but rather Fort Lauderdale. We called their dispatcher and we were told their bus driver had overslept and that they'd just sent down another bus, but because he was coming all the way from Fort Lauderdale, it was going to be close as to whether we were going to miss our flight home.

We called the airline and explained our predicament and we were told they couldn't wait for us, even though with a travel party of 45 people, we were probably at least 40 percent of the passengers on the flight. They did arrange for several streetside porters to be ready with our boarding passes and luggage tags already printed out so that as we unloaded the bus, the tags were put on the luggage and we ran through the terminal. No sooner had we sat down in our seats was the door closed and the plane departed. It was uncomfortably close and all because there was one person we forgot to remind about the time change: the bus driver. Live and learn.

When a Tankful of Gas Is Really Empty

My final van story is without a doubt my favorite. The last year I coached at Bucknell, we had a great group of women athletes. One weekend in early February, I took six of them to a last-chance qualifier meet at the University of West Virginia. Everything that could go wrong did go wrong.

We had a woman in the 5,000 meter run—roughly 3.1 miles for you metrically challenged folks—a triple jumper, a sprinter, and a relay team. All but the triple jumper were taken to this meet to try to qualify for the ECAC Championship—the women's equivalent to the men's IC4As. The triple jumper was there to qualify for the NCAA Championship.

The woman in the 5,000 was the first of our athletes to compete and she missed qualifying for the ECAC meet by four-hundredths of a second. In a race that lasts roughly 18 minutes, four-hundredths of a second is so close to qualifying without qualifying that I knew immediately after that race that we were in for a long day. The sprinter, who was also a member of the relay team we'd entered in this meet, ended up qualifying in the 55-meter dash but pulled her hamstring as she crossed the finish line, so we couldn't even run the relay team I'd brought. The triple jumper was the last to compete and she ended up missing the NCAA qualifying standard by two centimeters, which is less than an inch. Our objective for the meet was four qualifying marks. Our accomplishments: zilch.

We loaded up the van as a defeated group ready for the ride home, and about an hour into the trip, we stopped at a rest stop in the western part of the Pennsylvania Turnpike. We ate dinner, I filled up the tank, and we were ready for the ride back to Lewisburg. While we'd been eating, it had started to snow, and by the time we got back on the highway after dinner, the left-hand lane was closed to traffic, as the plows hadn't been out yet and the only reason why the right-hand lane was clear was due to the 18-wheelers blowing the snow to the side of the road as they sped by.

Within 10 minutes of leaving the truck stop, we were driving along, minding our own business, when a rock or maybe a chunk of ice no bigger than a fist appeared in the middle of the right-hand lane. I knew I couldn't pull out into the left-hand lane in order to avoid the rock/ice, as that lane was now covered with snow, so I decided to just drive over it, as it really was no bigger than a fist. Somehow, the suction of the van pulled the rock up and it hit underneath the van, making a loud noise. Loud, yes, but at the time, I didn't even give it a second thought.

Within a minute or two, one of the women in the back of the van asked me when it had started to rain. I told her she must have been asleep and dreaming, as it was snowing, not raining. But I did ask her what made her think that it was raining? She informed me that the back windows were dripping wet and at the exact same time I heard her say this, I looked down at the gas gauge and noticed that what had been a full tank only 10 miles previously was now the farthest left of empty I'd ever had the misfortune of seeing while in the driver's seat.

We'd obviously put a hole in the gas tank and I immediately knew that the engine at this point was strictly running on fumes. As luck would have it, we happened to be on the top of a hill with an exit at the bottom of the hill—rare indeed because in western Pennsylvania, the turnpike has an exit about every 40 miles. As we exited the turnpike, I paid the toll as the engine died. We coasted to a stop right in front of a motel at the foot of the exit ramp, which leads me to the next series of stories in this book: hotels and motels.

7
Motels

In my years as a track coach as well as my time in athletic equipment sales, I've spent an exorbitant amount of time on the road traveling to meets, recruiting, speaking at clinics, and attending conventions. Thankfully, as the years have passed, the level of hotels I've stayed in has improved, but back in the early days of my coaching life and once in a great while to this day, a dive of a hotel is unfortunately and unknowingly on the itinerary for an upcoming trip.

The Bates Motel

I left off the last chapter as the van was coasting off the Pennsylvania Turnpike with an empty tank of gas. As I paid the toll, I was relieved to see a hotel directly across the exit ramp from our van and fortunately there were enough fumes left in the tank to pull into the parking lot of the hotel. The neon sign out in front advertising "HOTEL" was in such disrepair that instead of pulling into a hotel, we were pulling into what the sign described as a "H EL." I should have realized right then and there we were in for a tough night and my initial relief upon seeing a hotel off the exit ramp was very short lived as we pulled into what the athletes would later refer to as the "Bates Motel."

I got out of the van and slid across the snow-covered dirt parking lot up to the office. It was probably 10 p.m., and as I entered the office, a loud barking dog came out from the back room—the kind of shabby dog made famous in horror movies. A TV was on in the back room, and as I rang the bell at the front desk, I was told "I'll be out at the next commercial." Fantastic, I thought. I'm dealing with a first-class businessman on this one. When the proprietor finally did emerge from the back room, he was dressed in the oldest bathrobe I'd ever seen, with the string tie undone, exposing open boxer shorts underneath.

I explained my dilemma to him and asked him if he had four rooms—one for me and three for the six women athletes. I was told in response that he had only two rooms, which were vacant. "Only two?" I asked, as I hadn't noticed a single car parked in the parking lot out front. "Yea, only two," he responded. "The board of health has condemned my other six rooms. How the hell am I supposed to stay in business with only two rooms?" "Oh my God" was the only thought I had. What was I supposed to do with six college women in a hotel that has had 75 percent of its rooms condemned? The women all checked into one room and I into the other.

Dirty sheets, no bedspread, and towels that looked as if they hadn't been washed since the last guest had checked out, but I was too tired to worry about it, so I left my clothes on, turned up the heat, and fell asleep on top of the bed, wrapping the pillow in one of my own T-shirts. When I awoke in the morning, I went out for a run, as we had to wait until a member of the university's physical plant arrived to fix the van. When I got back from my run, I decided to take a shower before our repairman arrived. When I opened the brown-stained and mildewed shower curtain, I couldn't believe my eyes, as there was a wooden pallet—one of those things used by a forklift to carry around heavy materials—on the floor of the shower. Thinking it had been misplaced, I went to remove it and realized that the reason the pallet was on the shower floor was because the shower's tiles were so disgusting that it had been intentionally placed there in order to keep one's feet off the floor. And this was one of the rooms that hadn't been condemned!

I was already sweating from my run and had no choice but to take a shower, so I put on my brand-new pair of running shoes and stood on the pallet, taking the only shower of my life that induced involuntary dry heaves. After my shower experience, I went to wake the women up and discovered that I'd been the lucky one, as their room was worse than mine because there was no pallet on the shower floor in their room, so none of the women had dared to set foot in the bathroom.

Finally, in the late morning, the Bucknell physical plant arrived with a tow truck and another van and we left the Bates Motel in a van with a full tank of gas as the tow truck dragged our van with a hole in the gas tank the three hours back to campus. As I checked out upon our departure, the proprietor still dressed in the old bath robe and same boxer shorts reminded us that we were always welcome back anytime. If I've ever visibly shuddered to my core, it was at the suggestion of considering returning to his hotel. I really do think we must have been the only guests he'd hosted in his hotel in quite some time.

Four to a Room

Oftentimes, when people watch big-time college football or basketball games on TV, the announcers regale viewers with glorious stories of the athletic department's facilities, equipment, and fringe benefits—sometimes even mentioning that the teams travel by charter flights or even on a school-owned airplane. To the uninformed viewer is oftentimes a perspective that all collegiate athletes are traveling via airplane, staying in five-star hotels, and eating in fantastic restaurants. Track isn't football or basketball.

When I was an undergraduate, I'm sure the track budget wasn't very substantial, so the majority of the time, our meets were within a couple hours of campus and we'd get up early in the morning, pack up the vans, drive to the meet, compete, and then return to school—all in the same day. An overnight trip for us was a unique and rare occasion—something which I'm sure we all looked forward to and I honestly believe appreciated. We certainly didn't stay in five-star hotels, but I'm not sure if many of the guys on the team would've known what to do or how to act in a ritzy hotel anyway.

My first overnight with the Colgate track team was an indoor meet at Lehigh University in Bethlehem, Pennsylvania. On the rare occasions we did stay overnight, we had to stay four to a room and our coach would put two upperclassmen and two freshmen in each room. The inevitability of this arrangement was that the upperclassmen would take the mattresses off the beds and relegate the freshmen to sleeping on the box springs. The upperclassmen would keep the sheets, pillows, and blankets and tell the freshmen, "Too bad—I had to sleep on the box springs without sheets or blankets when I was a freshman, so you do too." My first experience on a box spring was a nightmare, as the heat in the room was nonexistent and my upperclassmen roommates were oblivious to my predicament, so I froze my tail off all night.

So, there I was, a skinny freshman high jumper, sleeping on a box spring with no blanket and freezing in a room with no heat in the middle of January or February and I expected to compete the next day. The only analogy that I can come up with to compare my sensation from that night is imagining what it must feel like for a mountain climber to lose his sleeping bag and have to sleep in a tent in the snow with no covers in the midst of his climb. Needless to say, the freshmen on our track team never seemed to do very well at meets when we stayed overnight in a hotel the night before the competition.

NCAA Indoor Championship

In my first year of coaching at Colgate, the NCAA Division I Indoor Championship was held in the Carrier Dome in Syracuse, so our head coach and I volunteered to help organize the officials for the championship. Even though the schools are less than an hour apart, we decided to stay overnight in Syracuse because the meet was scheduled to end very late on Friday night and start quite early again on Saturday morning. My boss took care of the hotel arrangements and promised we'd be staying in a quality establishment.

After the meet ended on Friday night, we went out to have a few beers with some coaching friends of his and headed toward our hotel in the wee hours of the morning. We must have driven past the hotel entrance four or five times before we finally realized that the unlit driveway leading into the woods was indeed our hotel. We drove into the driveway and immediately knew we were in trouble. It was the worst hotel I'd ever seen because it actually wasn't even a hotel but rather a group of individual cabins tucked into the woods.

The cabin we ended up staying in had no hot water, a leaky roof—which we certainly wouldn't even have known about except it started raining quite heavily in the middle of the night—old linoleum tiles on the floor—which curled up in the corners—and, of course, cockroaches as long as your finger. Unfortunately, my only memories of my first NCAA Championship have nothing to do with the excellent competition but rather the poor housing and being seriously disappointed with my college coach's hotel selection.

Dogs, Dogs, and More Dogs

The first year I coached at Bucknell, we had a fantastic men's cross-country team. Our conference championship that year was held in Philadelphia and we stayed at a hotel in King of Prussia that has since been torn down. This hotel wasn't bad—a rather large complex of one-story buildings with each room having an entrance out into the parking lot—and if the truth be told, the only reason we stayed there was because the hotel also had a great sports bar.

There happened to be a big dog show out at the Valley Forge National Historic Park the same weekend as our conference championship, and unbeknown to us, our hotel was the only inn within 50 miles that had a policy allowing dogs in the rooms. When we checked into the hotel that Friday afternoon, we were obviously unaware of this policy and none of us gave it a second thought when we saw a few dogs in the parking lot while we were checking into our rooms. By the time we went to the site of our impending conference championship in order to run the course and later returned to our hotel, the parking lot and the rooms had turned into the largest kennel in U.S. history. I mean, dogs were everywhere: big dogs, small dogs, well-groomed dogs, dogs that looked identical to their owners—you name it, there was a dog to meet any and every description.

Every once in a while, we all have experienced a night in which one of the neighbor's dogs is barking constantly, thus ruining our night's sleep. Magnify that by a thousand and that's what we experienced that night. Barking, yelping, crying, howling—we heard it all and the front desk's response to our complaints was that this indeed was a hotel that allowed dogs on the premises and there was nothing they could do about it.

We won the conference championship the next day, although our kids looked a little ragged during the race due to sleep deprivation. On the bus on the way home, the kids all slept like babies. You've heard the expression "tired as a dog"? Well, that day, our team was tired from a dog—a lot of them.

Change Your Own Sheets

As I've moved up, down, and around the coaching ladder, I've had many work-related opportunities that are relevant to the sport but not related to the school where I'm employed at the time. Speaking at clinics and camps, traveling with elite-level athletes, going to other countries to give seminars, and being on the staff of U.S. national teams are just a few of these nonuniversity yet track-related experiences I've had. Normally, when someone asks me to speak at a clinic, the accommodations are very nice. A few years back, I was asked to speak at a weeklong clinic in the Midwest, and when I agreed to do the clinic, I was told it was a low-budget function, which I entirely understood, but I wasn't at all ready for how low budget this clinic was actually going to be.

The hotel that we stayed in that week was small and off the beaten track—a two-story building with about 10 rooms on each floor. I don't know what the proprietor of the establishment ate on a daily basis, but the odor from his kitchen was so overpowering that each of us commented that we thought we were going to pass out when we checked in. When we did check in, the owner informed each of us that he didn't have maid service in his hotel and that we were expected to bring our trash out to the Dumpster™ each day. He also informed us that if we wanted clean sheets or towels that we had to bring the dirty ones to the front desk between 9 a.m. and 10 a.m., exchange them, and then remake our own beds.

He insisted on the disposing of our trash each day and told us he'd check our rooms daily to make sure we'd thrown our garbage away. When one of the coaches asked the proprietor, "Wouldn't it be easier for you to empty our trash if you're already planning on going through our rooms to check the trash cans?" The owner responded by saying: "I own the hotel. It's not my job to empty trash." The coach wasn't ready to let it go and jibed, "If it isn't your job, then whose job is it?" The owner didn't like this particular line of questioning and informed the coach that if he didn't like the arrangements, he was free to find other accommodations. Not only was our hotel owner an unusual cook, but he certainly hadn't yet refined the better points of capitalism and running a quality business.

We naturally survived and thankfully for all staying at the hotel, the clinic started early each morning and ran late into the evening, so we didn't spend a great deal of time each day in this particular dump of a hotel, but one does have to admit exchanging sheets and throwing out one's own garbage are certainly not hardships but are also not expected when staying in a hotel.

Hookers, Pimps, and Moms

When I went from Bucknell to Syracuse, my life became significantly better regarding the modes of transportation and the style and quality of accommodations when traveling on the road with the team. Very nice upscale establishments became the norm for me, as our team traveled and stayed in a very professional manner. Well, most of the time anyway.

Quite frequently during the outdoor track season, we'd have two different meets on the schedule for the same weekend, as the better athletes on our team would fly to a fine quality meet in a warm weather environment and the rest of the team would bus to a meet a few hours from home and sadly compete in the relative cold of the Northeast in early spring. Our staff would always have a meeting over the summer to discuss the following year's schedule, and during that meeting, we'd assess the quality of the upcoming season's team. Based on that evaluation, we'd determine how many people we'd be flying to the warm weather meet and how many people we'd be busing each week the following spring. I'd then make hotel and plane reservations based on these estimates. One year, I dramatically underestimated our travel party for the Florida Relays in Gainesville.

Our team had competed much better that particular season than any of us had anticipated, and therefore, we had a much larger group of athletes who deserved to go to the University of Florida than I'd initially thought when making the hotel reservations back in August. In January, when it became apparent that our travel roster for that meet would be larger than I'd initially assumed, I called the Holiday Inn where I had our reservation and asked to reserve more rooms. We loved this Holiday Inn and had stayed there several years in a row, as it was right across the street from the campus and the athletes could walk to the meet and out for food. When I asked for more rooms, I was told that the hotel was completely sold out, as not only were the Florida Relays going on that weekend, but some annual motocross race called the Gator Nationals was also in town and the Holiday Inn and all their other local properties were sold out.

So, I called a friend of mine who happened to live in Gainesville and asked her to fax me a list of all the hotels in town (no Internet back then). After calling 17 different places, I finally found a hotel that had enough rooms available for our team. I then called my friend back and asked if this was an acceptable hotel for our team and was told: "Yes. As a matter of fact, my parents stayed there the last time they came to visit me." With her endorsement, I called back and reserved enough rooms for our entire group and cancelled the rooms we had at the Holiday Inn.

Before we departed Syracuse, I explained to the team that we initially had reservations at the Holiday Inn, but I had to change the reservation due to more athletes making the trip than we'd initially planned. I went on to explain that our only two options were to take less athletes and stay at the first hotel or bring everyone and stay in a hotel that we weren't familiar with. Everyone on the team understood that if we'd stayed at the former hotel that they all wouldn't have had the opportunity to go to the meet and that this was an acceptable alternative for all of them. Of course it was okay. People who live in Syracuse during the winter are willing to do almost anything to go to Florida in late March.

When we arrived in Florida, I knew immediately that either my friend's parents were not only blind and deaf but also must have lost their ability to smell or they were extremely understanding and tolerant people. The water that came out of the spigots in the bathrooms was brown, the sheets were dirty, and illegal activities were undoubtedly going on in several of the rooms on the backside of the hotel. I may be relatively naive to many things, but I know a pimp and prostitutes when I see them.

We ended up flying home on Sunday morning, and I thought that the trip and the bad hotel were in the rearview mirror. But Monday at practice, the mother of one of the kids on our team who happened to live locally came out to practice and accused me of negligence on behalf of her child. She even told me that her daughter normally slept in the nude, as that was the only way she could get a good night's sleep, but because the hotel was so dirty, she had to sleep with her clothes on and therefore didn't sleep very well. That certainly was more information than I needed to have about one of our athletes. When I explained the entire situation regarding having to switch hotels because of the increased number of athletes that we wanted to take to the meet and that if we'd stayed at the other hotel that we would've had to take fewer athletes and therefore her daughter probably would've been one of the athletes we left home, the mother told me that my explanation was irrelevant.

She went on to tell me that in the future, it was my job to check out the hotels our team was scheduled to stay in before we checked in and that if the hotel was no good, I should find a different place to stay and ideally I should check out all hotels in advance of our team staying there. We certainly didn't have the budget for me to fly each summer to the sites of all our away meets and check out hotels.

My response to all this was that the following weekend, we were making two trips: One was an 11-hour bus ride to William & Mary and the other was a plane trip to the University of Miami. I went on to explain that that her child was presently scheduled to go to the University of Miami—to a hotel we'd never stayed in before—whereas we'd stayed several times at the hotel in Williamsburg. "So," I asked, "are you telling me you want me to switch your daughter's meet this weekend to the 11-hour bus ride because we've stayed in that hotel before?" The mother's response: "Don't be a wiseass. You know damn well I want my daughter to go to Florida this weekend. Just make sure the hotel is nice enough that she can sleep in the nude." I rolled my eyes as the mom walked away and I realized you just can't win sometimes no matter what you say or do.

A Hole in Front of the Elevator

During my first year at Muhlenberg, the indoor ECAC Championship was at Wheaton College in Massachusetts. The Wheaton head coach and I have known each other since high school and over the years have served on several committees together. I called him during the fall and asked him for information on hotels near his campus, made reservations in September for the early March meet, and never gave it another thought.

The athletes and I made the six-hour drive from Pennsylvania and arrived a little after dinnertime to a totally vacant hotel parking lot. I walked in the front door of the hotel to discover that it was under renovation and that there wasn't a single person staying in the hotel. Remarkably, there was someone behind the front desk and I told her I had a reservation and she seemed almost in shock as she looked it up in her computer and discovered that I did indeed have a reservation.

Apparently, the sales manager had called everyone else that had a reservation other than me and moved them to other hotels. Because there was a big track meet in town, all the other local hotels were booked, so she suggested we stay on the one floor where renovations had yet to begin. We had no choice, so we went out to the van, grabbed our bags, and came back into the lobby. She gave us our keys and told us to be careful getting on the elevator. We walked down the hall to the elevator to see a four-foot- by three-foot-wide and three-foot-deep hole directly in front of the elevator. "We're jumpers," one of the athletes said. "We can jump over the hole and into the elevator." And that's exactly what we did—only to discover that the construction company was using this elevator to move equipment and materials up and down the floors of the hotel. As we jumped into the elevator, we ran directly into 10 to 15 two-by-fours with 16-penny nails sticking out of them.

Fortunately, the rooms themselves were fine and the kids competed quite well the next day. When I got back to school, I called the headquarters of the particular chain and explained the situation to them. A week or two later, I received several vouchers for free stays at their chain, so that spring when I was out on the road recruiting, I never had to pay for a hotel. I'll jump over a hole in front of an elevator anytime in order to get free hotel rooms.

I Need a Banana

My third or fourth year at Muhlenberg, we had a really great men's team at the Division III level. As a matter of fact, we came in 10th at the NCAA Indoor Championship that year. At the ECAC Indoor Championship, we ran the fastest distance medley relay (DMR) time in Division III in the country that winter, and based on that performance, the relay team qualified for the NCAA Indoor Championship. I'm really superstitious when it comes to the national championship and never make hotel reservations until the athletes have qualified, as I don't want to jinx our chances by being presumptuous and reserving rooms before anyone actually makes it into the meet.

The DMR qualified only six days prior to the national championship, so I didn't have a great deal of time to make travel arraignments before we left Allentown for DePauw University in central Indiana. All the hotels on DePauw's website were booked, as were all the hotels on the NCAA Championship website. I finally found a hotel about 15 miles away and took the final rooms they had available—site unseen and just thankful to have rooms less than an hour away.

The kids were really excited about going to the NCAA Championship and almost nothing could have dampened their enthusiasm. Nothing except possibly this hotel. One of my assistants on this trip happened to be an athlete at Bucknell when I coached there and also happened to be one of the athletes on the trip to West Virginia when I put the hole in the gas tank. As soon as we pulled into the driveway of the hotel, she immediately reminded the athletes and me about that wonderful experience from so many years before. Fortunately, the kids didn't let the hotel bother them and they performed extremely well and we came home with an All-American DMR as well as an individual all-American in the mile.

When we got back to the hotel after the meet was over, we all went into the room of two of the guys on the team. Their room was probably the worst of all the rooms we had, as there wasn't even a knob on the bathroom door. They'd gone across the street to the grocery store to buy a banana and then put the banana in the hole where the doorknob should have been in order to open and close the bathroom door. A rather ingenious solution to a rather unusual problem I must admit.

After realizing that the kids had to use a banana to get in and out of their bathroom, I decided to no longer allow my own superstitions to affect the team, so the following year, I started reserving rooms ahead of time.

8
Towns

One of the rather unique aspects of coaching track at the collegiate level is the opportunity to travel all over the country to compete. Football and basketball teams must routinely compete against the same schools year after year because they're required to compete annually against the schools within their own conference. Track teams don't have that same kind of restriction regarding scheduling, so oftentimes, coaches will purposely schedule different meets each year in order to expose the athletes on the team to various parts of the nation. Up to this point in my career, I've attended at least one track meet in 42 different states and attended either a track meet or a track clinic in eight different countries on three different continents. Through the years, I've seen many interesting things and met a variety of fascinating people as well as been to many unique towns and unusual places. This chapter is dedicated to several of the more interesting towns I've had the opportunity to visit.

Provo, Utah

One of the more unique towns I've had the good fortune of visiting is Provo, Utah—home of Brigham Young University. By no means are my feelings toward Provo meant to be anti-Mormon, but to the outside observer, the Mormon Church certainly does appear to control the entire community and I have no doubt that the entire flavor of the town is dictated by the church. I've been to Provo on two separate occasions. The first time was for the NCAA Division I Track & Field Championship back in 1989, and then a few years later, I was asked to return to Provo to teach at a weeklong track coaches' education school.

Provo is an absolutely beautiful city. Nestled into the foothills of the Rockies, the town sits right on the edge of the mountain range. When you sit in the stands on the home stretch of the track, you look straight up at an incredibly gorgeous set of mountains. The backside of the campus sits right at the bottom of the mountains and creates a mesmerizing and spiritual site for a university.

Robert Redford's famous ski resort Sundance is just a 15-minute drive from Provo, and both times I've visited Provo, I've driven to see the picturesque resort that's incredible to see even in the summer. Spectacular little ponds with cold, clean babbling brooks lead into them and the awesome set of mountain peaks are just remarkably inspiring. Even the gift shop is amazing and I understand that Redford himself personally picks out all the items that are sold in the store. Sundance is a peaceful place to visit and is a great spot to calm oneself before a major competition such as the NCAA Championship.

Of all the traveling within the Unites States I've been afforded the opportunity to take advantage of due to my job, Provo is the only city I've visited that has made me feel as if I'm in another country. This opinion may simply be based on the fact that the community is nestled in the Rocky Mountains and therefore gives off a bit of an Alps-like serenity. I don't believe the setting is the only cause for this sensation, though, as I think the citizens of Provo actually give off a vibe that may add to this perception. It may very well be my own paranoia, as the people of Provo are indeed very friendly and kind to visitors, but it's quite apparent that non-Mormons aren't always welcome in the community.

One evening during my first visit to Provo, several of my coaching friends and I decided to go out to a bar. A simple task in any city in America, right? Not in Provo it isn't. By all accounts, there were only two bars in Provo and one had a membership requirement, and because we were only in town for a few days, we ruled that one out. The other bar was a rather small facility right on the main street in town—big enough for two pool tables, about 10 tables, and a bar long enough for 12 barstools. The bar was directly next to a pet store, and because the noise ordinances in town are so stringent, the bar wasn't allowed to play music, so all one hears inside the bar are the dogs barking from the pet store next door. My peers and I went to this particular bar on several occasions during the NCAA Championship and the owner began to feel comfortable enough with us to tell some rather remarkable stories about the difficulties in running a bar in a non-alcohol-consuming society.

We all found it a tad farfetched, but the barkeeper told us that in Provo is a city ordinance that states it's against the law to carry on a conversation on a sidewalk in the downtown area after 11 p.m. and that the reason for this law is to put the bars out of business. According to the bartender, the ordinance was put into effect to discourage people from going into bars. Who wants to risk getting arrested because you were talking when walking out of a bar? Needless to say, we didn't talk as we departed the bar each night.

The bartender was quite adamant that the law had indeed successfully accomplished the lawmakers' objective, as he informed us that at one point, there were several bars in town, but the law had made the non-Mormons so nervous about drinking outside their own homes that all but two bars in town had gone out of business and the bar that we'd been frequenting wasn't exactly the Ritz. One night when we were in there, a mouse crawled through the wall of the pet store right into the bar.

The other time I went to Provo was to speak at a college track coaches' clinic. The clinic was eight days long, so at night, while the coaches who were attending the clinic were in their dorm rooms studying, those of us teaching the classes would make our way down to the aforementioned bar. We all became reacquainted with the same bartender from my previous visit to Provo and we also got to know the few regular patrons, as there were never more than three or four other people in the bar. The night before the last day of the clinic, we told the bartender there would be a rather large crowd the next night, as all the coaches who'd been studying quite extensively for a week would be coming out with us to celebrate the conclusion of the course.

Sure enough, the next night—our last in Provo—at least 100 college track coaches made their way down to the bar. We were all having a great time and I'm sure the bartender and waitress were probably working harder than they ever had to do in this bar. At one point, the owner of the bar walked in and took a look around his usually barren establishment and screamed out, "Praise Jesus, there is a God."

Earlier in the week on that same trip, I had another shocking experience in Provo. The clinic spanned eight days, which meant we'd be on BYU's campus on a Sunday. At BYU, the university basically shuts down on Sundays. Even outside groups, such as ours, weren't allowed to use the classrooms for teaching on the Sabbath. Not only was teaching out of the question, but any use of campus facilities was forbidden. We weren't even allowed to use the school's swimming pool even though it was the middle of the summer. Essentially, Sundays in Provo are set aside for the Mormon Church, even if you're not a Mormon.

Because we had nothing to do and we weren't allowed to use the school's facilities, several of us decided to take a walk around town. Because it was mid-July and quite hot, we all had on shorts and short-sleeved shirts. We were walking down the main street in town, minding our own business, when a well-dressed man in a very nice car slammed on his breaks, rolled down his window, and screamed at us, "Go to church, you heathens." We were all a little surprised by the outburst and it certainly did make us a little bit uncomfortable and clearly self-conscious about being there, but what were we supposed to do? There aren't many places in the United States where an American can be made to feel totally out of place, but that person sure made us feel as if we weren't welcome in Utah. Oh, well—live and learn.

Houston, Texas

In June 1989, the USA National Championships was held at the University of Houston, a great track facility and a wonderful setting for the USA National Championships. At that time, many of the greatest American track stars—Carl Lewis and Leroy Burrell, to name a few—were living and training in Houston, so the local fans came out in significant numbers to support the meet in general and their local heroes specifically. The meet itself was a great, but it was my exposure to a shocking side of Houston that I most vividly remember.

The meet was many years after the energy crisis of the mid-1970s and years before the horrifying disaster of the hurricanes in the early 21st century, but in the late 1980s in a community where oil had been king forever, the oil crisis of the 1970s had clearly devastated Houston. I don't profess to be an economist nor a businessman, but I did indeed see a significant amount of suffering in Houston due to America's dependence on oil. Houston has indeed revitalized itself since then, but back in the 1980s, Houston was in an economic transition and not copping with it very well.

We stayed at a beautiful hotel in downtown Houston and the drive to the university was no farther than five miles. The route that the concierge suggested we take from our hotel to the competition took us through some neighborhoods that absolutely blew my mind. Within just a few short blocks of the campus were homes that I can honestly state only had three exterior walls. These poor people didn't have four walls in their homes and their houses were totally exposed to the elements. I'm not speaking about one or two homes either. I'm talking about entire blocks where the poverty was incredibly rampant, and except for three out of four walls, people were for all intents and purposes living outside.

If that weren't enough of a shock, one night during the course of the competition, a friend of mine invited me to go with him to a party that he'd been invited to. My friend had gone to graduate school in Houston and had met many of the big supporters of track and field in the Houston area while he was a student there. One of the women who was officiating at the championships was married to a rather influential banker in the area and she'd decided to throw a party for the officials and coaches who were in attendance at the meet.

An amazing affair and a beautiful home, the party was in the banker's backyard under tents. Fully catered with fine foods and a totally stocked bar, this was one of the finest homes and one of the most upscale parties I'd ever attended. At some point during the evening, I went inside the house to use the facilities and the host's husband introduced himself to me. When I explained I was a coach at Syracuse University, he told me that he'd grown up back east and had been an Orange fan in his youth.

He subsequently gave me a private tour of his home and I was in awestruck. I'm not sure what the term is for the level above awe, but whatever it is, I reached that plateau when we entered the living room and he showed me not one but two original Picassos hanging on the wall. I don't know anything about art, but I was certainly aware that I was looking at a great deal of money hanging there on the wall, and being the consummate skeptic that I am, I was thinking to myself, "This man has two Picassos in his house and he's having a party with his house wide open and he doesn't even know who's on the guest list."

As we drove back to our hotel, we were all amazed at the wealth, power, and hospitality in the home we'd just left. We couldn't have been five minutes away when we went through the poverty-stricken neighborhood I previously mentioned. That's the epitome of going from the sublime to the ridiculous. Never before and certainly never since then have I gone from such an extreme in such a short period of time—one minute partying in a multimillion-dollar home and the next driving by three-sided shacks.

On our last night in Houston, a group of us decided to go out and celebrate the conclusion of the meet—a night I'll never forget. The throws coach at Syracuse had just been named the U.S. women's national shot put chairperson and we decided to take her out to celebrate and coincidentally it also happened to be the birthday of one of the other members of our track coaching staff. So, we loaded up the van with several nationally ranked throwers—none of whom weighed less than 250 pounds—and off we went to explore the night life in Houston. I agreed to be the designated driver that night, so I had the opportunity to sit back and watch the show.

Our final stop of the night was a rather large nightclub that actually had three different bars within the club. One room was a country-and-western-themed bar with a band playing in it, another room was a quiet place with pool tables, couches, and bar games in it, and the third and largest room was more in the mode of a New York City nightclub with a dance floor. There must have been 15 to 20 people in our group and all had been drinking rather heavily for quite some time when our birthday-celebrating coach jumped up on the shoulders of the reigning U.S. hammer champion and challenged anyone in the bar to a chicken fight. Hammer throwers are rather large people, and other than a few joking attempts by the others in our group, thankfully no one took him up on his challenge. Needless to say, though, we were asked to leave the bar.

We left the bar with surprisingly little fanfare and I began my journey as the designated driver. I took a group back to our hotel first, as the majority were staying there and this was also the loudest group in the van. I then had to take six or seven people to other hotels all over Houston—I'm sure none of which would've been easy to find during the day with a sober passenger giving me directions, let alone with a group of rather trashed individuals. I eventually ended up returning everyone to their proper hotels and arrived back at my hotel about an hour and a half after I'd initially dropped the first group off. It must have been around 3 a.m. by the time I reached my room—only to discover that the person I was sharing the room with was nowhere to be found and we had a 7:30 a.m. flight.

I was about to call security when I heard a rather feeble attempt being made to unlock the door. I went to the door and carefully opened it and there was my roommate standing it the doorway, soaking wet with nothing on but his underwear. When I asked what in the world had happened and where his clothes were, he responded with a drunken giggle: "When we got back to the hotel, I wanted another drink, so I went to the bar next to the pool. The bar was closed, but I knew some guys were still in the bar and we decided to go for a swim." So, at 2 a.m., after already having a chicken fight in a bar, my roommate decided to go skinny-dipping with a bunch of guys he barely knew.

After convincing him to dry off, force himself to throw up, take a couple aspirin, and drink some water, he finally passed out—only to be awakened two-and-a-half hours later so we could catch our plane. Never have I been more thankful to have been asked to be the designated driver, as I'm sure as we headed to the airport those that had been out with us the night before were wishing they were dead.

I explained earlier when writing about our van breaking down somewhere in northern North Carolina or southern Virginia that we used to go to a lot of last-chance qualifiers at the end of the season to make a last-ditch effort to get our athletes into the NCAA Championship. The year after the Chapel Hill fiasco, we convinced our head coach that it would be much safer if we flew somewhere rather than driving, so we headed back to Houston to a meet titled the Meet of Champions. The individuals entered in this meet were outstanding and we were sure we'd come to the right place to ensure our athletes would qualify for the NCAA Championship.

In mid- to late May in Houston is apparently a chance of rain daily, but we were told that even if it did rain, it would only last for a few minutes and that the rain in the forecast wouldn't impede the start of the meet. The weather report seemed to be correct, as the meet started on time and the sky was blue. Shortly thereafter, though, it started to come down in buckets. At one point during the course of the evening, the lightning was so close to the track that it hit the light towers around the stadium. We waited and waited and waited, but it never stopped raining, and as always seems to be the case, the locals were continuously saying, "It never rains in Houston like this." Well, I've got news for them: Yes, it does—and I saw it.

The NCAA rules committee has very strict rules regarding the very last opportunity to qualify for the national championship. This rainy night was indeed the very last day to qualify, so the head track coach at the University of Houston called a friend of his on the rules committee and explained the situation, inquiring if he could move his meet to the next afternoon. The response from the rules committee member was a rather disappointing "Yes, you can have the meet tomorrow, but none of the performances will count toward qualifying purposes." Naturally, as we departed for home the next morning, the sky was blue and there was no rain in the forecast.

We didn't have any vans break down on the trip, but at least the year before, even though it was the trip to hell and back, the kids had the opportunity to compete, whereas this year, we'd spent a significant amount of money to fly out to Houston, and for the first time ever, a meet at the University of Houston was rained out.

Baton Rouge

Of all the towns in North America I've had the pleasure of visiting, Baton Rouge, Louisiana, is without a doubt my favorite. The food, the hospitality, the music, and the bars are all fantastic. I love Cajun food and there's no place better than Louisiana's state capital for out-of-this-world bayou cooking. Admittedly, it doesn't have the flare of New Orleans, but all the ingredients for a great time and great food are in the town that's home to the LSU Tigers.

There are just too many great restaurants in this town to count, and no matter how many times I've gone to Baton Rouge for a track meet or a meeting, I've been taken to a wonderful place to eat. Even the gas stations and mini-marts in Baton Rouge have great food. A little Ma and Pa beer and convenience store is across the street from the LSU track and field complex and it has great takeout. Every time I've gone to a track meet at LSU, I've walked across the street to this place, picked up four or five pounds of crawfish, and sat in the upper deck of the stands to watch the meet and enjoy this delicacy that you can't find anywhere else on Earth other than Louisiana.

Long before I knew about the great culinary wonders of this community, I made my first trip to Baton Rouge. I was coaching at Bucknell at the time and LSU was hosting the NCAA Outdoor Championship. Our head coach and I had wanted to go to the meet, and when none of our own athletes qualified for the championship that year, we were on our own to travel to the meet. The NCAA pays the travel and per diem for all coaches and athletes who qualify for the meet, but without a qualifier that year, we weren't eligible for the reimbursement. So, along with a friend of ours who was coaching at Columbia University, we decided to drive from Lewisburg, Pennsylvania, to Baton Rouge.

Our friend from Columbia had the voice and accent of the classic stereotype of a person who'd grown up in Brooklyn. His very thick "hey, yo" voice still oozed out of his vocal chords despite the fact that he hadn't lived in Brooklyn for years. We packed up a Bucknell University school-issued station wagon on a Monday morning, filled it with an air mattress, a sleeping bag, and a cooler, and departed Lewisburg. I realize that college kids from across the country annually pack up their cars and road-trip 18 to 24 hours during their spring breaks in order to drink and sleep on a beach, but we were grown men, not used to all niters, and determined to reach Baton Rouge by sunrise the following day.

The trip was a pretty easy drive from a directions standpoint, as we got on Route 81 in Harrisburg and drove due south. Our intention was to pull down the backseat of the station wagon and have one person sleep in the back while one person drove and the third person was responsible for sitting in the front seat and keeping the driver company. Things went along for quite a while as planned. Our first stop was shortly after we crossed the border between West Virginia and Tennessee. Tennessee back then was a state that still allowed the sale of firecrackers and fireworks, and the first exit we came to after crossing the border was infested with little fireworks stores. We stopped at some old firetrap named something like "Crazy John's Fireworks Store." The store appeared to be ready to go up in one quick explosion worthy of a Harry Truman A-bomb the minute anyone contemplated lighting up a cigarette within 100 yards of the store.

We were like three kids in a candy store. I'd never seen my boss so excited as when we set foot in the store. I guess we were all junior pyromaniacs at heart and this store with row after row of legalized explosives was just too much for us to contain ourselves. Crazy John's totally threw us off our entire travel itinerary, as we must have spent an hour or two in this store drooling over the prospects of what it would be like to purchase the items in the store. After an hour of browsing, though, we decided it would make more sense to stop at this store on the way home so we didn't have explosives in our car for five or six days.

Off again we went on our trip, leaving Crazy John's behind for another day and continuing on with what was turning more and more into a mission rather than a leisurely trip. We drove well into the night—through Tennessee, Georgia, Alabama, and Mississippi. At one point in the wee hours of the morning, we stopped for gas and food somewhere in the heart of Alabama. I'm not aware of the initial reactions people have when they see what they think is a UFO or an extraterrestrial, but when we walked into this gas station in Alabama at 2:30 a.m., I think the other people in the store thought for sure they'd seen one or at the very least heard one. Our friend from New York started to ask the person behind the counter about something in the store and the stares from the few other patrons in the establishment when he started to speak with his accent clearly indicated that these people had never heard anything like this in their lives. A Brooklyn accent in the heart of Alabama in the middle of the night was a very rare occurrence indeed.

We gassed up and headed back out again on our journey, leaving behind a shopkeeper loaded to the hilt with stories about the strange accent he encountered on his night shift working at a truck stop. As the youngest, I ended up drawing the night shift driving duties, and as my two companions immediately fell asleep, I drove into the night. Essentially, when you drive to Baton Rouge from the north, you go to New Orleans and then go west on Interstate 10 for an hour through the bayou. Somewhere between New Orleans and Baton Rouge, the sun began to come up as I was driving. I'd been up for most of the time since leaving Lewisburg 20 hours earlier and had been driving in the dark for at least the last four or five hours. As my two travel companions slept, I saw something I've never seen before and hope to never see again as a pink elephant ran across the highway right in front of our car. Even though we were only a half an hour from our final destination, I pulled over and begged for someone else to drive, as I was extremely tired but was still rational enough to realize that even in the Deep South, they don't have pink elephants and maybe I should stop driving.

We finally pulled into Baton Rouge on Tuesday morning, and as we pulled into the parking lot of our hotel, a friend of ours who was the head women's coach at Penn State University was returning from his morning run. As he went to say hello, he looked at our car with "Bucknell University" written on the side and at the Pennsylvania license plate and just laughed and said, "You've got to be kidding me?" I'm sure it was a great meet, although I don't remember any of the details of the competition itself, but one thing I do remember was the coaches' banquet. The meet director had arranged for the majority of the local Cajun restaurants to serve their best dishes in a buffet-style setting. This was my first exposure to great Cajun food and thankfully not my last. Our friend from Columbia University was allergic to shellfish and not realizing that almost all Cajun food is full of shellfish, he began eating hardily at the banquet. He was also totally bald, and at one point during the evening, his head turned bright red and the sweat began to pour off his head as if someone had turned a sprinkler on. Fortunately, he was fine and we had a wonderful time the rest of the evening, but I'll certainly never forget the stir his red head caused.

We went to the meet all day Wednesday, Thursday, and Friday and had a great time during the course of the first three days of the meet and the competition was scheduled to begin on Saturday—the final day of the meet—at 6 p.m.. We checked out of our hotel at 1 p.m., went for lunch, drove over to the meet at around 5 p.m., and, as had been the case the three previous days, enjoyed the competition thoroughly. At 9:30, the meet ended and I'd suspect every coach and athlete in attendance went back to their respective hotels, relaxed, and got a good night's sleep before heading home on Sunday. Not us. We got back into the station wagon at the end of the meet and headed home.

As on the way down, we stopped in Tennessee at Crazy John's, and this time, we bought our fair share of explosives for the upcoming Fourth of July. We continued on after that stop in Tennessee in a rather quiet manner, as I'm sure at this point we were all contemplating the exact same thing: "What in the world had we been thinking when we first came up with this rather suicidal trip idea?" I vividly remember crossing the border between Virginia and Maryland and all of us being rather excited that we were "almost home." But we still had at least four more hours to go—since when is four hours from home "almost home"? We finally made it by mid-afternoon on Sunday, and remarkably enough, our friend from New York turned down the invitation to stay in Lewisburg for the night and continued on the rest of the way home. The things we'll do to watch a track and field meet!

Dinner in Albany

At Colgate, most of our competitions were one-day trips and frequently held at off-hours due to the availability of the host institution's field house. Normally, college track meets are on Saturday afternoons, but when I coached at Colgate, many of the schools we competed against shared their indoor tracks with the basketball teams. Therefore, our meets were oftentimes relegated to Friday nights or Sunday afternoons. One such meet was an annual triangular meet against the University of Vermont and Union College hosted by Union, which is in Schenectady, New York, a suburb of Albany.

This particular meet was on a Friday night and historically didn't end until well after 11 p.m. While the athletes were showering after the meet, our head coach told me to take a van and go buy some food before all the local restaurants closed. He gave me several hundred dollars and told me to go to a fast-food restaurant and buy enough food to feed the 50 people on the trip. On the main strip near the campus was a plethora of fast-food joints but all of them were closed by the time I left the field house. I finally came to a Burger King® that still had its lights on, so I got out of my trusted van and walked up to the front door just as the manager was locking it up for the night.

He saw I was alone, so he unlocked the door and invited me in to order what he obviously thought was an order for one. I went up to the counter and some teenage, minimum-wage, acne-faced high school kid asked me what I wanted to order. When I told him, "Fifty Whoppers®, 50 large fries, and 50 Cokes®," he responded with a cynical, "No, really, mister, what can I get you?" When I told him I was serious, he called over the manager and explained to him my order and quite obviously the manager was equally as skeptical as the young clerk and he told me: "You have one last chance to seriously make your order or get out of here. What are you, drunk? We don't have time for games at this time of night!"

At this point, I pulled out three $100 dollar bills, placed them on the counter, and again told them I wanted 50 Whoppers, fries, and Cokes. As I was placing the order, I could see the employees in the back finishing up their cleaning ritual for the evening, as they were finishing up mopping the floor, scrubbing the grill, and completing their other daily chores before closing. When I put the money down on the counter, the manager had no choice but to take my order. I heard an infinite and continuous chorus of swears from the back as the employees were asked to fire up the grill and cook my order. I was quite relieved to be able to bring back food to the team, but I was also a little nervous about the group of upset employees behind the counter and whether they'd be diligent in properly preparing my order. Needless to say, they weren't happy with their manager or me for this extra duty they were now being asked to perform. They slapped those burgers together so fast and so haphazardly that despite my hunger after the long meet, I chose not to eat my share of the food on the way back to campus. I didn't dare tell anyone on the team how rapidly and carelessly the order was prepared.

Bermuda

During my sophomore year of college, our track coach arranged for the team to spend our spring break on a training trip in Bermuda. When our coach first proposed this to us in a team meeting the previous fall, it sounded too good to be true and everyone on the team immediately cancelled any and all spring break plans and opted for a trip to Bermuda instead. What our coach told us was the following: The Bermuda track and field federation wanted U.S. college track teams to come down to their island to compete against their national team. These meets gave their team a chance to have some quality competitions and qualify for major international meets, such as the Caribbean Championship, with little or no adverse effect to their national team budget.

In return, the federation promised free housing and a free lunch every day for all on our team. Because the team always went on a spring trip—albeit a van trip to Virginia, not a plane trip to Bermuda—there were budgeted funds to pay for our other meals and some of the transportation costs. If I recall correctly, each one of us had to pay somewhere in the neighborhood of $150 to $200 to go on the trip. It indeed sounded too good to be true, and as it turned out, it was too good to be true. We landed at Bermuda's only airport on a sunny, warm, and humid spring afternoon, having left behind snow and subfreezing temperatures in New York. When we departed the airport and got on the bus, everyone on the team was extremely excited with anticipation of our week ahead in the tropics.

We drove into Hamilton, the main town and the capital on the island, and the bus stopped right downtown. Yes, we thought, our housing must be fantastic because we're right on the main street. But as Lee Corso frequently says on ESPN College GameDay, "Not so fast, my friend." We got off the bus, and low and behold, a ferry was waiting for us. Perplexed, we unloaded the bus—only to have to load our stuff onto the ferry, and we were shipped out to a little island in the middle of the main harbor. There was only one building on the island—a rather large structure with a wraparound porch, one large room, and a kitchen on the first floor and one room underneath in essentially what amounted to the basement. There were approximately 30 cots in the main room and the basement—no single rooms on this trip.

Each cot had an old, moldy mattress on it, with no sheets or pillowcases. The mattresses were so old that each one of them was wrapped in some kind of plastic casing like the ones parents put on children's beds when they have a bedwetting problem. No one had ever informed us to bring sheets or sleeping bags, so we were destined to sleep for a week on plastic without sheets or blankets. Some of the guys actually cut a slit in the plastic covering and used it as a sheet and slept on the moldy mattresses. I still cringe when I think about that. As it turned out, this was our free accommodations. As college students, my teammates and I had always lived by the motto "Never turn down a freebie." For the first time in my college career, the motto may have been wrong.

It wouldn't have been too bad, but the ferry only stopped at our island three times per day: 8 a.m., 3 p.m., and 8 p.m. So, now not only did we have to spend a week sleeping in a room with 30 other guys on beds with no sheets, but we were essentially trapped on the island. We adjusted, though, and by the second day, everyone began to figure out our way around and how to time the ferry rides correctly.

The other thing our coach had been promised was free lunch for everyone on the team each day. What this was in actuality was a bribe to keep college kids off the majority of the beaches. Each of us was given a ticket every day for lunch, as was every college student on the island enjoying their spring break. The ticket was good for lunch on a particular beach each day that was established ahead of time. There would be a band and games on the beach—sort of a pre-MTV spring party weekend concept—and in exchange for your ticket, you could wait in line for an hour and receive a hot dog, a bag of chips, and a soda. This was our free lunch. The Bermuda Chamber of Commerce created this arrangement in order to keep all the college students in one locale. Apparently, the hotels would then warn their other guests as to which beach not to go in order to keep their more important, full-paying vacationers away from the rowdy college students.

Upon our arrival in Bermuda, our coach had given each of us our allotted meal money for breakfast and dinner for our week on the island. I've forgotten how much he gave us, but it was probably no more than $10 per day. Anyone who has ever vacationed on a Caribbean Island knows that $10 a day just isn't going to cut it. You can barely get a piece of toast and a glass of orange juice in Bermuda for $10. So, on our second day on the island, our coach collected all the meal money back from us and he and our athletic trainer went to the grocery store and bought enough peanut butter, jelly, bread, cereal, and pasta to feed us for the week. He then set up a duty roster to establish some of us as daily cooks and some of us as dishwashers. I was on the cook roster the first night, and as we were searching through the kitchen for pots to boil the pasta, we were scared half to death when a family of three rats jumped out of one of the kitchen cabinets. This trip got better and better at every turn.

Several of the guys on the team were beginning to meet people at the noontime beach parties and were getting quite frustrated as their newfound friends continually regaled them with stories of the great night life on the island while we were trapped on our own island with no way to get out after eight at night. Our coach hadn't established a curfew for us because he knew we had no choice but to be on the last ferry. One night, though, after our coach had fallen asleep, several of the guys decided to go ashore. They'd left a change of clothes and a towel underneath the dock on shore and swam the 400 yards to Hamilton. This wouldn't have been too bad except our island was right in the middle of the main harbor and there were always cruise and cargo ships steaming by at all hours of the day and night. After their night in town, they swam back to our island via the moonlight, with ships passing right by them.

When all was said and done, we ended up having a great time in Bermuda. The training aspect of our trip went really well, the team had a great season that spring, and despite the drawbacks of standing in line for lunch every day, sleeping on mold, dealing with rats, and having to take a ferry to bed, our coach really went the extra mile for us on that particular trip.

Tornadoes and Track Meets

The year after we went to Bermuda, it was back to reality for our track team on our spring trip. I don't remember all the details of the trip, but I do remember we ended the trip with an outdoor track meet at Lehigh University in Bethlehem, Pennsylvania, the first or second weekend in April. Not the tropics.

Because Bethlehem is only a few hours from where I grew up in Connecticut, my mom decided to drive to Lehigh and watch the meet. We had a small dog that weighed no more than 25 pounds, and as the team got off the bus, I saw my mom and our dog walking across the parking lot toward me. The morning of the meet turned out to be cold and gray, and at one point, the wind came up so strong that the dog was picked right up off the ground and knocked over. It was really windy! Lehigh has an indoor track right next to their outdoor track, so many of the events were contested indoors, and as a high jumper, I was one of the fortunate few who was able to compete indoors and not contend with the brutal weather outside.

One of the big goals for everyone on our team each year was to qualify for the IC4As. The IC4As is actually the oldest track meet in the world, dating back to the 1880s when it served as the U.S. collegiate championship and even predates the modern Olympic Games. After the NCAA was formed, though, the IC4As evolved into the Eastern Championship.

In order to qualify for the IC4As, an athlete had to meet a predetermined standard in any one single meet during the team's regular season. Well, with the wind as it was that day, there was very little chance that anyone was going to qualify at Lehigh, but the host school's coach decided to switch the direction that the sprints and hurdles were contested in order to run with a tailwind rather than a huge headwind. We had a hurdler on our team who was good, but he'd never qualified for the IC4As before this weekend, and with the poor weather conditions, it didn't appear as if he would on this day either. When the gun went off for the 110-meter hurdles, a huge gust of wind came up and not only did he qualify, but he qualified with the fastest time in the East that spring.

On the way home in the vans, we heard on the radio that the Lehigh Valley had encountered a series of tornados that day and several had been spotted within a mile or two of the Lehigh track facility. We always joked after that meet that our hurdler didn't just have a wind-aided time for his personal best but actually had a tornado-aided performance. One year, we were on the beach in sunny Bermuda, basking in the picturesque scenery and warm surf, and the next year, we were fighting to stay upright in the foreground of a tornado. Once thing I can say for certain about college track: In a brief period of time, you can be exposed to significant extremes.

Disneyland and Throwers

During my second year at Syracuse, the USA National Championships was held in Norwalk, California, a suburb of Los Angeles. We had six or seven athletes qualify that year for the national championships, and because the meet was at the end of June and we were out of school, we were able to go out to California several days before the meet started. Many people involved in international athletics contend that in order to adjust to time zone changes, athletes should arrive at the site of a competition one day early for each time zone changed. The meet started on a Wednesday, so we went out on Sunday. The group of athletes we had with us included a discus thrower, two hammer throwers, a shot-putter, a couple hurdlers, and a long jumper. Athletes who compete in the throwing events in track and field tend to physically be the largest athletes in the sport, so needless to say, we had some rather large individuals with us on the trip.

After dinner on Sunday night, I asked the kids if they wanted me to take them to Disneyland the following day. Several of the athletes said yes, but the throwers all said no, and I could tell by their response that they thought that they were too cool or too mature to go to an amusement park. On Monday morning, I called back to our campus to inquire as to whether it would be an NCAA violation for the school to pay for the kids' admission fee to the park and I was told it was an acceptable expense in the eyes of the NCAA. So, before we departed, I informed the throwers that I'd pay for them to go to Disneyland. Needless to say, they all changed their minds and decided they did indeed want to go.

I've been to Disneyland on three separate occasions and must admit I've never considered myself too old, cool, or mature to enjoy a day at the Magic Kingdom. Very shortly after arriving at the wonderful and exciting venue in Anaheim, the kids discovered the exact same thing about themselves. We were walking through the park with little kids as excited as they'd been in their short lives and our group of young adults who a day earlier were too cool for Disney became increasingly enchanted with the thought of going on the rides.

We did it all—the Pirates of the Caribbean, the Matterhorn, and even It's a Small World. We went on everything. The thing I remember most, though, was Space Mountain: these huge guys—all acting as if nothing could scare or intimidate them—getting off that ride and looking like ghosts. They were all excited and as giddy as children and just thrilled with the moment. At the end of the day, they each even wanted their pictures taken with the likes of Mickey Mouse, Goofy, and Roger Rabbit. What a thrilling day we had and to think that the ones who ended up having the most fun were the same individuals who were the most skeptical about going in the first place.

I took several freshmen to Disneyland a few years later when the Junior National Championships was also in Southern California, and unfortunately, it wasn't nearly as much fun. I think half the fun that day several years earlier was watching the transformation of the throwers from questioning whether they even wanted to go to the point of having so much fun that they didn't even want to leave at the end of the day. Life is full of surprises. Even when you think you've seen it all, something new will happen to make you realize that all of us are truly kids at heart when it comes right down to it.

The White House

The same trip that took us to Chapel Hill and ultimately a broken-down van in southern Virginia started a few days earlier in Washington, DC. We had arrived back home from the IC4As on a Sunday night and had left for Georgetown University on Tuesday morning. We arrived in Washington by mid-afternoon on Tuesday, and after an afternoon workout, we were pretty much free until Wednesday night's meet. Several of the athletes on this trip had never been to the District of Columbia, so on Tuesday afternoon, we went on a little sightseeing excursion.

We visited the Lincoln Memorial, the Washington Monument, the Jefferson and Vietnam memorials, etc. The highlight for the athletes, though, was definitely the simple walk we took around the sidewalk that serves as the perimeter of the White House. I'm sure that the sidewalk has all kinds of safety monitoring systems in, above, and underneath it in order to protect the President's residence, and if anyone was listening to our kids as they walked around the perimeter of the home at 1600 Pennsylvania

Ave., they'd have had quite the chuckle. Here I was with seven or eight college-aged kids, who the majority of the time appear as if they know it all and are incredibly mature. Well, on this particular afternoon, they were all just totally in awe of being that close to the White House. As I said earlier with regard to the kids we took to Disneyland, it's wonderful to see them get excited about something that I normally would've expected them to treat as either no big deal or not even care about seeing. As I said earlier, sometimes college kids can really amaze me with their levels of excitement and enthusiasm.

Buses in the Bronx

I wasn't a participant in the following story, but it happened to a high school cross-country team from the Syracuse area when I lived there. The team's unfortunate experience was very well documented in the local newspaper shortly after it happened.

Van Cortlandt Park in the Bronx has the oldest cross-country course in the United States. The park is situated in the northwest corner of the Bronx—just below Manhattan College—and it essentially serves an identical purpose for the citizens of the Bronx as its more famous city park counterpart—Central Park—does for residents of Manhattan or Prospect Park in Brooklyn. Dating back to the late 1800s, this park has hosted many of the greatest cross-country meets in American history. College races, high school races, national championships, and local races have all been hosted on the famed course. Everyone who has run cross country on the East Coast has run at least one race there during his running career and it almost serves as a badge of honor to be able to say you've raced there.

The park isn't just for cross country, though, and one of the really unique aspects about Van Cortlandt is that the city parks commission won't allow a race to have sole possession of the park during an event. The start of the course is in a very large, open field, and on any given Saturday during the cross-country season, the beginning of any race requires the runners to contend with no less than youth soccer games, Pop Warner football games, a few rugby matches, possibly a cricket game or two, and even a dog obedience class. All these unusual obstructions for a cross-country race really add to the ambiance of the course.

It really is a thrill to go to a race there, as it's truly like a three-ring circus. Oftentimes, more than one race is going on at the same time, as the high school and college courses don't use the same starting line, so it's entirely possible that two different races will go off simultaneously and then flow in together in the back in the part of the course known as Cemetery Hill.

One fall Saturday back in the early 1990s, one of the high school teams from Syracuse went down to a big high school invitational at Van Cortlandt Park. They departed Syracuse on Friday afternoon, stayed in a hotel in New Jersey the night before the race, and then drove over the Hudson River on the George Washington Bridge the morning of the race. The two things the park lacks are ample parking and available changing facilities. Parking a bus on Upper Broadway is a challenge for even the most experienced bus driver, and subsequently, the kids must change and store their personal items on the bus, as you can't do it anywhere else.

The high school team from Syracuse did all the requisite aspects of running at Van Cortlandt: struggling to park on Broadway, changing on the bus, leaving all their personal effects on the bus, and then heading out to run. The runners ran their races, and after warming down, they loaded the bus for the four-and-a-half-hour ride home. The only problem was that when they got back on the bus, the bus driver was nowhere to be found and all their luggage, clothes, and other personal items were gone. Hours passed and the team still didn't have a driver to take them home. At one point, the coach called back to the bus company in Syracuse to inquire if anyone knew the whereabouts of their driver and, of course, they didn't.

Finally, the bus company sent two drivers all the way from Syracuse down to New York to pick up the team and their bus. The team arrived back in Syracuse some nine hours after they were supposed to and without their clothes, which had obviously been stolen when the bus driver mysteriously vacated the bus.

A few weeks later, the truth was revealed. The team's bus driver was originally from New York City and had left the bus unattended all afternoon to go see his family. By the time he realized how late it was, he knew he was in trouble, so he just decided not to return to the bus. When he went to find the bus later that night, he discovered it was gone and figured the company had sent down another driver to pick up the team.

What the driver hadn't counted on was the bus company filing a missing person's report with the New York City police department, as of course they were nervous about the safety and whereabouts of their driver. The driver was discovered by the police a couple weeks later in New York, living with his family. It was never revealed what the bus company did—if anything—to the obviously recently fired bus driver, but one thing is for certain: The poor kids never did get the items back they left on the bus during the race.

I still take teams to Van Cortlandt every year or two and always stress to them the importance of not leaving their items unattended. Call it paranoia, but I always request a bus driver I'm familiar with when we make this trip, as I certainly want to be assured that the driver won't depart the bus. I never want to have our athletes stranded in the northern section of the Bronx like those poor Syracuse kids were several years ago.

9
Equipment

This certainly wouldn't be a fully descriptive documentation of the life of a college track coach without the inclusion of stories regarding the sport itself. Believe it or not, sometimes the track equipment itself leads to unfortunate incidents.

Pole Vault Poles

To say the least, pole vault poles can be rather cumbersome, as they range anywhere from 12- to 16- feet long and a single athlete might use up to three or four different poles in a single competition. A team with three or four pole vaulters may very well travel with upward of 10 to 12 poles. Most schools own a pole vault bag, which is essentially a large vinyl bag capable of holding 10 poles. When full, one of these bags is 16-feet long with a diameter of about a foot. This rather large piece of equipment can be a real pain in the rear end when a team is on the road.

When a team is traveling by van, it has essentially three potential options for transporting poles. The first is to rest the poles on the driver's side mirror, tie the other end of the poles to the hinge of the back door of the van, and then wrap a towel or rope around the middle of the set of poles, bringing the towel inside a window in the middle of the van and then shutting the window. If the team doesn't have great vaulters and thus the poles aren't very long, it's possible that if the poles are shorter than 13 feet that they'll fit inside a 15-passenger van, resting on the dashboard and extending all the way to the back door of the van. And finally, the poles can be tied to the top of the van.

I've witnessed problems with two out of these three methods of pole transportation. During my freshman year of college, we went to an away meet with the poles resting on the side view mirror, tied to the back door, and secured with a towel wrapped around the poles and then securing the towel inside the window. It was a rather cold and raw day outside and the entire drive to the meet was in a mixture of snow, rain, and sleet. By the time we arrived at the meet, the towel was totally frozen, and even though the ropes that were tied to the front and back ends of the poles were easily removed, the poles remained resting on the side of the van, hanging on the frozen towel.

No matter what any of us did, we couldn't get the window open, as the wet frozen towel had somehow locked the window in a closed position. Finally, one of the members of our team suggested a light tap on the window may loosen the ice up enough to enable us to open it and subsequently free the frozen towel. The light tap didn't work nor did a little bit harder of a tap, but a rather aggressive young man decided to really give the window a good swat to see if he could free the frozen towel. Crash went the window and, yes, the poles were now free from the van, but we now had a van without a side window in the middle of the winter two hours from home. Needless to say, it was a long, cold ride home.

We went to St. Lawrence University every winter for an indoor meet and one of our pole vaulters had been improving that season, so the coach bought him a bigger pole in order for him to continue to jump higher. Up to that point, he must have been on a 13-foot-long pole throughout his career, as we had always put his poles in the inside of the van. When we left campus that afternoon, we must have had plenty of time to pack and the guys responsible for the poles must have either tied them to the side or the top of the van. We drove the two-and-a-half hours north, stayed overnight, got up the next morning, competed in the meet, and then showered in preparation to go home.

College students are always in a hurry to get moving and head home after a meet, especially one where the team stays overnight, as missing one night of fraternity parties is bad enough, but the prospects of missing an entire weekend of them is unimaginable. So, when the pole vaulters came out to tie their poles to the van, someone already inside said: "Just put them inside like we always do. I'm in a hurry to get home. Stop wasting time trying to tie them on." So, we opened the back door of the van and slid the poles in, forgetting that one of our vaulters had gotten a new pole that was six inches longer than the others. Pole vault poles have a rubber plug on the end that vaulters plant into the pole vault box when taking off. The back door was slammed, and because the pole was six inches longer than the length of the van, the plug went right through the windshield and we now had a one-inch diameter hole in the windshield.

Just as with the broken side van window, we now had a two-and-a-half-hour ride home in the middle of the winter with a hole in the windshield. These problems naturally never happened during the outdoor season on a nice sunny warm afternoon but always in the middle of the winter. Understandably, after breaking two windows in vans in one winter, we were no longer allowed to carry the poles any way other than tying them to the roof.

Poles on a bus are much easier to haul around than in a van. The easiest way to store them is to open the front passenger side window of the bus and then push the poles through the open window and store them on the floor in the aisle of the bus. Windows on most coach buses don't slide but rather open from the bottom and swing up toward the top of the bus, as the hinges are on the top of the window. A hinged lock at the bottom of the window must be secured after the window is closed in order to lock it back in place.

We were heading out on a four- or five-hour trip one time and whoever put the poles on the bus neglected to relock the window securely after putting the poles on the bus. Whoever was sitting in the front seat must have been leaning against the window for the first 15 or 20 minutes of the ride and not noticed that the window wasn't locked. The bus driver had already gotten us onto the interstate and was probably going at least 60 miles per hour when the front seat passenger leaned away from the window. The combination of the lock not being secure, the pressure inside the bus, and the speed we were traveling immediately unhinged the window and it swung outward and upward and slammed onto the top of the bus, breaking the window into a million pieces. Talk about scary. I don't think anyone initially realized what had happened and I think everyone on the bus thought we were under attack. The bus driver did a great job of keeping the bus under control as he decelerated and eased the bus off the road and onto the shoulder. He called back to his bus depot and told them what happened and we just sat on the bus for an hour or so waiting for a new bus to arrive. Then, we unpacked our windowless bus and reloaded the new bus—this time making sure the window was secure after putting the poles on the bus. As I said earlier, hauling pole vault poles around can be a real pain in the rear end.

Sand in the Long Jump Pit

Long jump pits are filled with sand for two different yet equally important reasons. Sand leaves a permanent mark when someone lands in it, so it's easily determined where the athlete landed for measuring purposes during a competition. Sand is also a soft material that gently moves with the athlete when he lands in it after making an attempt, so it helps to prevent injuries and offer a nonabrasive landing area from a safety standpoint. Most people can certainly see the rationale for having sand in a long jump pit—from a safety and competition standpoint.

I worked at a school at one point in my career that had racquetball and squash courts right next to the long jump pit in the indoor track. The athletic director and the president of the college enjoyed playing each other in squash quite regularly. One afternoon, the president slipped going after a ball during his squash match with the athletic director and sprained his ankle pretty badly. The athletic director was understandably upset—not in a compassionate manner regarding the president's injury but rather toward the track coaches for leaving the long jump pit uncovered.

He came storming into our office immediately after his match with the president and started yelling at us and blaming us for the president's sprained ankle. "If you didn't have sand in that pit," he said, "the president never would've slipped, as I know there were granules of sand from your pit on the floor of the squash court." We didn't even know what he was talking about at this point, and after our head coach calmed him down, we learned that the president had been injured on the squash court right next to our long jump pit. Our head coach then asked: "Well, what do you suggest we do about it? We water it once a week and have a tarp over it to keep the dust down." "Remove the sand" was the athletic director's response. "You only have sand in the pit for the kids to land safely in anyway. Take the sand out and replace it with foam rubber chips."

We all kind of looked at each other thinking the same thing: "Did the athletic director just tell us to remove the sand in the long jump pit? Does he not realize that the reason for sand is to measure the jumps correctly during meets?" The head coach then said just that to the athletic director. The athletic director's expression was priceless as the lightbulb went on in his head and he realized how stupid he'd just sounded to the track staff. "Oh, right. Well, just make sure this doesn't happen again" was his parting statement as he walked out the door. Our entire staff sat in utter silence after he left, as we were all totally amazed at the lack of recognition of a key part of our required equipment by our immediate superior.

Hammer Throwing and Basketball Just Don't Mix

In track and field terminology, the hammer is an event contested by throwers. The implement itself is a ball the size of a shot put, weighs 16 pounds for the men and 8.8 pounds for the women, and is connected to a handle by a thin steel wire. The total length of a hammer is almost four inches from the top of the handle to the bottom of the ball—without a doubt a deadly implement if used incorrectly. The origin of the majority of the throwing events in track and field date back to ancient wartime weapons and the hammer is no exception.

To throw a hammer successfully, a right-handed athlete must wind the ball counterclockwise around his body, with the ball reaching its highest point off his left shoulder and its lowest point at off his right foot. Once the athlete has the ball moving around the body at an acceptable velocity the athlete must then spin his entire body around—also in a counterclockwise direction—as he moves his entire body from the back of the hammer circle toward the front. A great athlete can spin four times around between the back and front of the circle in order to get the ball moving at an incredible rate of speed, as the velocity of the ball ultimately determines how far the athlete is capable of throwing the hammer.

Most outdoor throwing venues have a concrete slab near the throwing circles, which enables the athletes to work on footwork and various drills for their event without actually throwing the implement. A practice slab is particularly beneficial for hammer throwers, as they really need to perfect the winding of the ball around their body and then subsequently spinning their body up to 1,340 degrees while continuing to wind the ball around their body. Many hammer throwers will daily practice the winding of the ball and the spinning of their body while holding the ball.

One year, we had an exceptionally bad winter and still quite a bit of snow remained on our throwing field after the outdoor season had begun. Because of the excessive snow, our throwers were unable to practice outdoors. Not a big deal for the shot-putters, as they were able to throw indoor shot puts in our field house. We also had a tarp hanging over a set of bleachers that would allow the discus throwers to throw indoors into the net. It was difficult for the hammer and javelin throwers, though, as it's clearly impossible for them to throw their implements indoors.

Our throws coach came up with some rather ingenious solutions, though, as the javelin throwers would throw weighted balls, plastic javelins, and pieces of bamboo in the field house to try to replicate the throwing of a javelin the best they could. Unfortunately, his solution for hammer practice wasn't quite as wise as his mock javelin throwing. He decided it was perfectly safe for the athletes to practice their hammer winds and their hammer spins in the field house as they normally would've been doing outside on their practice concrete slab.

The problem with this decision was, as we soon found out, hammer throwers will oftentimes let go of the hammer handle after doing a series of winds rather than slow down while still holding the hammer. Certainly fine if you're out in a field with no one else around but not such a great idea if an entire track team is practicing in the same facility.

If you've ever watched a basketball game on TV, you know that the basketball hoops in most major facilities operate on hydraulics and fold down when not in use. When folded down, the backboard is perpendicular to the ground and the top of the backboard is no higher than shoulder height. We had about eight of that kind of basketball hoop in our field house and thank God the basketball team wasn't practicing when our coach had the hairbrained idea of doing hammer turns in the field house.

One of our hammer throwers was practicing her spins with a hammer extended out in front of her when she clearly forgot she was inside and, as she'd done hundreds of times outdoors, she let go of the handle as she was slowing down. Our entire team stopped working out and watched in horror as an 8.8-pound ball was traveling across our field house at a pretty high rate of speed at waist height. The good news was that it didn't hit anyone; the bad news was that it went right through the glass backboard of one of our basketball hoops. The amazing thing was that the ball went right through the backboard—not breaking it but rather putting a hole in it the exact size of the hammer. A huge sigh of relief was felt as the ball came to a rest on the other side of the basket and no one was injured.

We all went over to the basket in utter amazement and stared at the hole. Within seconds, the backboard began to turn into a giant glass spiderweb, and as soon as one person touched the backboard, the entire glass part crashed to the ground in a million pieces. By now, the news had made its way to the facility manager's office and she came out to inquire as to what had just happened. Once she was assured that no one was injured, she took the throws coach aside and calmly yet firmly asked, "You're not planning on doing that in here again, are you?"

Of course, he never did that again, and thankfully, we never again dealt with a flying hammer in our field house. Once was certainly enough for that particular brand of excitement.

Call the Fire Department

The steeplechase is a rather unusual event in the sport of track and field. It's a race of 3,000 meters—a little bit less than two miles or approximately 7.5 laps on an outdoor track. Each lap includes four 3-foot high barriers as well as a fifth barrier that includes a water barrier that's 12-feet long, 12-feet wide, and 3.25-inches deep. The event is grueling and is a true test of endurance and athleticism, as the competitors need the fitness of a distance runner and the agility of a hurdler.

Before 1992, USA Track & Field would sponsor a national championship in outdoor track every year. In 1992, the decision was made to no longer sponsor a national championship during an Olympic year, as they concluded it made more sense to have the Olympic Trials serve as not only the team selection for the Olympic Games but also as the national championship every four years and strictly host a stand-alone national championship during the other three years.

In 1988, though, there was a national championship as well as an Olympic Trials during the same summer. The national championship that year was in Tampa, Florida, and because it was only a few weeks earlier than the Olympic Trials, many of the athletes who thought they were going to make the Olympic team either didn't compete in the meet in Tampa or didn't take the competition very seriously. I don't think anyone was really taking the meet too seriously, including the meet organizers.

Many steeplechase water pits are covered for safety purposes when not in use. Some facilities leave the pit filled with water even when not in use; others believe that for safety purposes that they should always be empty even if they're covered. An hour or so before the men's steeplechase was set to begin, the meet organizers uncovered the water pit for the first time all week—only to discover no water in it.

Twelve-feet wide by 12-feet long by 3-feet deep is a lot of water and certainly not something that can be filled in an hour with a hose. The meet organizers came up with a quick and successful idea and called the fire department. Minutes later, a fire truck rolled out onto the track—with the meet suspended for the duration of time that the vehicle would be out on the track—and we all watched in fascination as several men who are normally putting out fires and protecting our property were being asked to fill up a water pit.

It worked and the meet continued without a hitch, and I'm sure the members of the local fire company had a pleasant story to tell about how they'd used their equipment on that particular afternoon for something far less dangerous than putting out a fire.

Football Headsets

A Division I regular season football game called the Mirage Bowl (and later the Coca-Cola Classic) used to be played in Tokyo, Japan. It was annually contested at the beginning of December as two teams' last regular season football game. During my tenure at Syracuse, our football team was invited to play in the Tokyo game. The school administrators spent the entire fall planning the big trip abroad. All the players needed passports, the team needed to charter a flight, classes needed to be rescheduled, and hotels and meals needed to be arranged.

The equipment manager had a huge responsibility on his shoulders that fall, as he needed to pack not only the team's game uniforms but also practice equipment, as the team was going to be in Tokyo for several days before the game and would obviously need to practice while they were there. Normally, when the team competed in a regular season away contest, he would've just packed the game uniforms and equipment and warm-ups for the day prior to the game's walkthrough practice. When the team went to bowl games, the practice equipment was shipped, but at least the bowl games were within the United States and either the equipment went on the plane with the team or it was packed in a rental truck and driven to the destination. Because the game was in Japan, all the equipment for a normal bowl game had to go with the team without the advantage of shipping it by truck.

The team left for the Saturday game on Tuesday or Wednesday, and after flying for nearly 20 hours, it arrived in Tokyo. The following day, the equipment manager was taken out to the stadium by one of the members of the local organizing committee and was shown where all the team's equipment was being stored. He searched through every crate to make sure that all the equipment had arrived safely, and following his diligent checklist routine, he discovered that the coaches' headsets were missing. Football coaches at any level can't function on game day without the headsets, as this is their only line of communication between the coaches on the sidelines and the coaches in the press box.

The equipment manager panicked and went through his entire checklist a second time, but he still couldn't find the headsets. He was adamant he had packed them, but he succumbed to the fact that they weren't there. "No problem," he thought. "We're in the electronics capital of the world. We can buy new ones." No such luck—the value of the U.S. dollar versus the yen at the time was so poor that it made that option fiscally impossible. He finally decided to inform the administrators on the trip that the headsets were missing and that he'd already discovered that purchasing new ones was an impossibility.

He called one of his assistants back on campus and asked him to search for the headsets back in the athletic department's equipment room. "No," his assistant informed him, "they're not here. I only found the old headsets the coaches used two years ago." The decision was made to ship the old headsets from New York to Japan, as it was significantly cheaper to ship the old ones rather than buy new ones. The only problem with this idea was that by the time the decision had been made to ship the old ones, it was Friday in Japan and it would take 24 hours for the headsets to arrive and the shipping company's receiving center in Tokyo wasn't open on Saturdays and therefore wouldn't be able to be retrieved until Monday—a full two days after the game.

The next idea was to just put them on a commercial flight bound for Japan, but none of the airlines were willing to allow the school to ship the crate of headsets on their flights without a passenger along with the package. Therefore, it was down to a final option: Send someone with the headsets.

So, on Thursday morning (New York time), an unsuspecting assistant equipment manager at Syracuse came to work without the slightest knowledge as to what his next 72 hours were about to be like. He was drinking his morning coffee when one of the assistant athletic directors inquired if he had a valid passport. He affirmed that he did indeed have a valid passport and proceeded to ask why. "We need you to fly to Tokyo with the headsets. Your flight leaves in two hours" was what he was informed by the administrator.

He went home, picked up his passport and needlessly packed some clothes, went back to the office, picked up the headsets, and was taken out to the airport. The good news, as he discovered when he arrived at the airport, was that because the ticket had only been purchased an hour or two before, the cost difference between coach and first class was so nominal that the school had paid the additional cost and he'd be flying all the way to Japan in first class. The bad news was that, including the return trip, he'd be on an airplane almost nonstop for the next two and a half days.

He'd later admit, "The flight was so long and because I was in first class the whole time, I was able to get drunk, fall asleep, sober up, and then get drunk again at least three or four times on my way there." He finally arrived in Japan and was met at the airport by a member of the school's athletic staff. They loaded the taxi with the crate of headsets, and according to the staff member and the assistant equipment manager, "We really stressed to the taxi driver the importance of getting us to the stadium as fast as possible." Both agreed that the taxi driver took them at their word and it was the most dangerous cab ride either of them had ever been in.

They arrived at the stadium an hour and a half before the game began—only to be stunned at the discovery that had been made that morning. The organizing committee had removed both teams' headsets from the rest of the equipment when the team arrived several days earlier in order to set them up for game day. The opposing team had somehow known this was the case, but the language barrier had prevented our equipment manager from learning this until the morning of the game. His assistant had just flown 24 hours for nothing.

To make matters worse, the school was starting final exams the following week, so the team itinerary called for the team to eat dinner right after the game and then board the charter flight back to the states, and because the school had only purchased a one-way ticket for the assistant equipment manager, he was expected to return home with the team on the charter flight. He never even had the opportunity to change his clothes, as he was assigned the responsibility of returning to the airport with the head equipment manager and all the team's belongings right after the game ended in order to have the charter plane packed and ready to go when the team was done eating dinner.

He ended up spending no more than six hours in Japan and more than 48 hours on a plane over a period of two and a half days. He was a mess for at least a week afterward, as I don't think his body knew up from down and certainly had no idea what time it was for several days to come. All for a set of headsets that were never even used.

10 Meets

Surprisingly, the majority of the humorous situations I've encountered during my 25-plus-year career as a coach have happened off the playing field. Luckily, the meets generally go off without a hitch, and despite infrequent weather delays, I've experienced very few nonathletic memorable moments at meets. As a friend of mine who owned a track timing business was fond of saying to me: "Don't worry about it. I've never been to a track meet that didn't end." He was correct—at least most of the time.

Maybe It Will Rain

As I mentioned earlier, our men's basketball team made it to the national championship game one year (1996) while I was coaching at Syracuse. During the first or second round of the tournament, I was out watching the game with some friends and the team was losing at halftime. I was so frustrated that I went home and watched the game by myself and sat alone in utter excitement as they made a huge comeback and won the game, advancing on to the next round of March Madness. I've been known to be quite superstitious, and for the remainder of the tournament that year, I made sure I watched the first half of the game with other people and the second half by myself.

The track team happened to be at the Florida Relays in Gainesville the weekend of the Final Four and the majority of the kids on our team were as excited as I was about the run the basketball team was experiencing. The only problem we had was that the meet was scheduled to end on Saturday night at around 7 p.m. and our men's basketball team was playing in the national semifinal game at 5 p.m., so there was no way we were going to be able to watch the game. Halfway through the afternoon, the skies absolutely opened up and the rain came hard and steady for at least an hour. The track was entirely underwater and not a single athlete on our team was disappointed when it was announced that the remainder of the meet was going to have to be cancelled.

The Final Four that year consisted of Syracuse vs. Mississippi State and Kentucky vs. the University of Massachusetts. Kentucky and Mississippi State are both members of the Southeastern Conference—the same conference that the University of Florida is a member of. Because the Florida Gators weren't competing in the Final Four, as this was pre-Billy Donovan and therefore pre-Florida basketball success, the majority of the people living in Gainesville were rooting for the two SEC schools and against Syracuse and Massachusetts.

We arrived back at the hotel soaking wet and giddy with excitement that we were going to be able to watch the game. Earlier in the week, I'd noticed that the hotel bar had a huge TV, so when I arrived back at the hotel, I asked at the front desk if it would be all right for our team to watch the game in the bar even though most of the kids were under 21. We were given permission, so 40 wet young adults clad in Syracuse track uniforms and the coaches went into the bar to watch the game. There were probably 20 to 30 people in the room watching the game when we walked in and it was quite apparent they were rooting against Syracuse. They sat quietly, realizing what school we were affiliated with and remarkably never once said anything derogatory to us and eventually got caught up in our enthusiasm. It was great to see the kindness and respect they showed our team as they cheered on their friends.

Of course, I had to maintain my self-imposed solitude for the second half, as clearly my actions had a huge impact on the team's success. At least, I was convinced that that was the case, so at halftime, I went up to my room. Our lead widened and widened as the second half continued and it became more and more apparent that we were going to make it to the national championship game. Everyone on our team was staying on the same floor in the hotel, and during a TV timeout with about eight minutes to go, the kids who had been watching the game in their rooms rather than in the bar were running around the hallway screaming with excitement. Tongue in cheek, I ran out into the hallway and screamed: "Will you guys keep it down? I'm trying to watch *Family Feud*!" Several of the kids knew I'm a college basketball junkie, although one of the kids mumbled under her breath: "Is he serious? He's not watching the game? Doesn't he know we're on TV right now?" It was priceless. A coach will never pray for a meet to be cancelled, although this particular weekend was as close as I ever came to being thankful that we were able to go back to the hotel and watch the game rather than competing ourselves.

Banked Tracks and a Lightning Storm

Indoor tracks come in all shapes and sizes. The standard distance for an indoor track is 200 meters, although back in the day—when the major indoor venues, such as Madison Square Garden, hosted a lot of meets—many facilities had 160-meter banked board tracks that would fit inside the perimeter of the hockey rink. Schools started to build field houses in the 1960s, and initially, the tracks were 160 meters, but as schools built better and better facilities, 200-meter indoor tracks became the norm. The next wave of technology brought about the advent of 200-meter banked tracks.

A banked track is flat on the two straightaways and the two curves are banked in order to make the track faster. Some banked tracks are suspended, having been built on a frame all the way around, so the track itself may be a foot or so above the ground. This makes the track extremely fast, as the energy the surface gives the athlete during each and every stride is exceptional. Other banked tracks are only suspended on the curves and the remainder of the track is actually poured onto the existing floor of the building. Either way, running on a banked track for the first time can be a rather unique experience and a level of technique is clearly required for an athlete to master the bank.

One of my first solo experiences as a coach was to take a group of four athletes from Bucknell to a prestigious meet at the Meadowlands in New Jersey in the arena where the New Jersey Nets and the New Jersey Devils played their home games. Our head coach gave me specific instructions as to where to park, where to pick up the information for our race, where to get the runners' competition numbers, etc. He had me prepared for everything as I entered the building for the 4x800 meter relay—the race we were to run that night. Our level of expectation was extremely high and the four guys were really competing in the race with the intent of winning.

Banked tracks in indoor facilities like the Meadowlands are 160 meters. All the field events, such as the high jump, long jump, pole vault, and shot put, are contested in the infield, so not only is it a three-ring circus but also a rather congested three-ring circus. The long jump and pole vault pits came right up to the edge of the track and one had to be very careful not to get run over.

The gun went off for our race and our leadoff leg went right to the front. He ran his 800-meter leg perfectly and flawlessly and handed off the stick in first place. Our second leg did exactly as he'd been instructed and our lead grew as his leg continued. Our third leg got the stick in the lead and again widened our lead. Then, I couldn't believe my eyes: Our third leg ran right into the pole vault pit on the edge of the track and landed on the pit. By the time he recovered, three or four teams were ahead of us as he struggled to finish his leg. By the time our anchor leg got the stick, we were in second-to-last place and that's exactly where we finished.

I called our head coach, and before I could explain what happened, he asked, "What do you mean they came in second to last?" After I explained the situation, I thought for sure I was never going to be given another opportunity to take the kids to a big meet. Thankfully, that wasn't the case, but seeing someone bounce off a pole vault pit in the middle of a race is certainly memorable.

During my second or third year at Muhlenberg, we had a really good men's 4x800 relay and we were convinced we were going to win the Eastern Championship in that race. The meet was at Boston University—which has a suspended 200-meter banked track—so the track was about a foot off the floor all the way around the oval. Our anchor leg got the stick in the lead and was clearly feeling the pressure of winning the race. Instead of going out at a moderate pace and maintaining the lead, he instinctively tried to widen the lead from the outset. He ran the first 600 meters of his race at least at a pace five to six seconds faster than he'd ever run the 800 in his life.

The crowd was oohing and ahhing, as they didn't know we were running too fast, and our lead got wider and wider as the race progressed. With about 100 meters to go in the race, it became pretty apparent that he'd gone out too fast and his legs started to go slower than his upper body was demanding and he began leaning farther and farther out in front of his legs. With about 50 meters to go, his legs just gave out and he fell right off the track and somehow rolled underneath the track. He got up pretty quickly and our lead was so large that only two teams caught us, but I've certainly never seen someone lying underneath a track in the middle of a race. As I said, a learning curve is definitely needed for running successfully on a banked track.

One year at the outdoor ECAC Championship, we had a rather outstanding female distance runner entered in the 5,000 meters run—a distance of about 3.1 miles. The weather looked rather ominous leading up to her race, but the meet was already behind schedule, so the meet director decided to start the race. Almost exactly halfway through the race, a thunder shower that would've shocked Noah himself came rolling across the track facility. The meet organizers had no choice but to stop the race in the middle.

It's one thing to stop a 100-meter race in the middle and expect that the athletes can return later on in the day and run successfully, but it's another thing entirely to expect someone racing for more than three miles to do so after stopping the race halfway through. It's always frustrating to take an athlete to a big meet like the one in the Meadowlands or the Eastern Championship and not do well, but to have the race fail because an athlete fell into a pit or under the track or to have the race stopped in the middle due to lightning can be devastatingly disappointing. Mistakes on banked tracks or lightning during a race—I hope I never see either one of them again.

You're in Baltimore?

We hadn't reached the era of traveling by bus during my first year at Muhlenberg, so our mode of transportation back then was still via vans. We usually had enough kids traveling to warrant three 15-passenger vans and we'd ordinarily travel in a caravan to our away meets. I'd always explain to my assistants the route we were going to take just in case someone got a little bit behind, but normally, we'd follow each other the entire way. Normally.

One Saturday morning, we were traveling to Messiah College, which is just outside Harrisburg. One of my assistants had never been to Messiah before, so I explained the route to him: Route 78 West to Route 81 South to Route 83 to Route 15 South and then follow the signs for Messiah—simple. Shortly after we got on Route 78, he had to go to the bathroom, so he pulled off at the next exit and stopped at a gas station. By the time he got back on the highway, we were long gone.

As we neared the exit off Route 83, I discovered it wasn't Route 83 to Route 15 but rather a route in between for about a mile and a half that connected 83 to 15. Route 83 has no signs for Route 15—just a sign that reads "To Camp Hill/Gettysburg." "No problem," I thought. "Everyone knows that Gettysburg is on Route 15. He'll realize to take that road to get to 15." At that intersection, Route 83 heads south to Baltimore, which is about 90 minutes south of Harrisburg.

We arrived at the meet, the kids warmed up, and the meet started, but there was still no sign of our one assistant and his vanload of kids. This is before everyone had cell phones, but one of the kids did have one and called a friend in the lost van. My assistant got on the phone with me and asked: "How far down Route 83 is this exit for 15? We're only 15 miles from Baltimore?"

I informed him of my mistake in the directions I'd given him and I've never heard someone swear so loudly into a phone in my life. He had to turn around, backtrack an hour, and finally got to the meet about halfway through. Fortunately, the majority of the kids who were in the van were still able to compete in their events, but I don't think my assistant talked to me for at least two weeks. Now I always double-check my directions twice before we head out on the road, as I never want that to happen again.

Military Academies

I've been lucky enough to go to track meets at the Naval Academy and the Military Academy, and I have to say it's always quite a thrill to drive onto the campuses and soak in the history, beauty, and dedication that ooze from both campuses. Not only is it an honor and a privilege to be accepted and attend the Army, Navy, or Air Force academies, but I also think it's an honor to compete against them on their campuses.

We used to go to a meet every year in Annapolis at the Naval Academy, and one year, we were unable to secure a hotel for our entire team. We called the head coach at Navy and asked if he knew of any hotels that could handle our entire roster and he told us not to bother—we could stay on campus in Ricketts Hall, an old dorm that was used to house visiting teams. We were none the wiser, so we took him up on his offer.

The cots were clearly as old as the academy itself and appeared to date back to the Civil War. They were just incredibly uncomfortable. Naturally, the showers didn't have hot water either. Talk about an inhospitable situation and a home-court advantage—Ricketts Hall was it. Then, to add insult to injury, the freshmen—or, as they're known at an academy, the Plebes—do their morning marches at about 5 a.m. directly out front of the visiting team dormitory.

When we arrived later in the morning for the meet, our head coach questioned the housing environment with the Navy head coach and he kind of slyly grinned and said: "Gee, I'm sorry. I had no idea there was no hot water. We certainly never would've suggested you stay there if we'd known that the beds were so poor." I wondered how many times had he said the exact same thing to visiting coaches over the years. He knew exactly what the situation was and he certainly got the better of us that weekend, as Navy beat us quite soundly. Needless to say, we never stayed on campus again after that experience.

The Military Academy is in West Point, New York—right on the Hudson River. The campus is spectacular and the views of the river from the campus are breathtaking. The outdoor track is right on the river, so early spring meets at the Military Academy can be rather cold and blustery. We competed in a meet there one year that was really bad, as the wind and rain were really strong and we were actually a little surprised that we continued with the competition.

Back in those days, track meets were timed with a piece of equipment called an AccuTrack. AccuTrack was essentially a really sophisticated Polaroid® camera with a timing device inside it that was triggered to start when the starter's pistol was fired. The camera would then take a picture as the athletes crossed the finish line and then the automatic time was able to be matched up on the photo with the athlete's torso.

In order to achieve the correct angle of the finish line for the camera, the device would have to be mounted on top of scaffolding about 10 feet off the ground. An individual would have to sit with the camera all day, removing and replacing the film after each race.

On this particular day, someone had neglected to secure the scaffolding to the ground, and if the day had been mild, it wouldn't have been a problem. But the winds on this Saturday afternoon were anything but mild and it was very unsafe for anyone to operate the AccuTrack. When you go to a track meet at an academy, a lot of officers are always around and the AccuTrack operator that day was no exception, as he was a full-bird colonel.

During the course of the meet, the wind became worse and worse, and at one point, the scaffolding started to rock back and forth. With each rock, the legs were getting a little bit higher off the ground and the distance of the rocks was getting slightly wider. An AccuTrack costs about $4,000, and I think as the scaffolding began to rock, most people would've either climbed down or jumped off the scaffolding to save themselves. I don't think that ever crossed the colonel's mind. A huge gust of wind eventually knocked the scaffolding right over and the colonel and the AccuTrack fell from 10 feet in the air.

The colonel still didn't jump off but rather grabbed the AccuTrack and tried to protect the piece of equipment rather than protect himself. He was injured quite seriously and we discovered later that he suffered a compound fracture in his leg. As he was lying on the ground, clearly in a great deal of pain, he looked up at one of the other officials, gritted his teeth, and asked, "Major, did I save the AccuTrack?"

Only at a military academy will you ever see that kind of toughness out of a track and field official. It certainly made me realize right then and there the level of commitment, dedication, and sacrifice the members of the U.S. military are willing to do if that's what one of them will do for a piece of track and field equipment.

11

Facilities

Maintaining a college campus from appearance and population standpoints is clearly big business. Schools must be fiscally responsible and operate in the black on an annual basis. One way for schools to ensure proper enrollment annually is to have a pristine campus, as renovated and updated facilities are a must in today's business of running a campus. I've been involved in college athletics long enough to have been around many athletic facility renovations and construction projects. If Murphy's Law absolutely rears its ugly head in any area, it's on construction sites.

I'm Fired?

The year before I arrived at Muhlenberg College, the school renovated the football stadium and track. Out went the cinder track, grass football field, and wooden bleachers and in came a state of the art track, an Astroturf® football field, and brand-new bleachers and lights for night games. The school was obviously proud and pleased with the new facility and everyone on campus was very excited about the recent transformation.

Somewhere along the line, an employee of the track-surfacing company informed the school administrators that athletes wearing spikes on the track would decrease the life expectancy of the track. The employee of the surfacing company was in all likelihood referring to casual users of the track, not the track team itself, although he apparently neglected to differentiate this to the administrators.

When the construction project was completed, signs were placed on the fence surrounding the facility with such obvious restrictions as "No Dogs Allowed," "No Smoking," and "No Bikes on the Track." An additional sign placed on the fence read "No Spikes Allowed."

My first year at Muhlenberg was the second year for the facility, and during the first year, the coaches on the track staff made the assumption that the signs referred to outside users, not members of their team. One day, an administrator happened to be out on the track during practice and noticed that the kids were changing their shoes during practice. He went over to one of the assistant coaches standing near the shoe-changing athletes and inquired as to what they were doing. "Oh, our relay team is getting ready to practice stick exchanges, so they're putting their spikes on to replicate a meet situation" was the assistant's response. He didn't give it another thought.

When he got back to his office, he had a message on his answering machine from someone quite high up in the school's hierarchy informing him that he'd demonstrated an entire lack of respect for school facilities and therefore his contract was immediately and permanently terminated. He hurriedly sought out the head coach and explained the message, and by the next morning, the issue had been resolved and he retained his job, but I'm sure this is the only time a track coach has ever been fired for asking his athletes to wear track spikes.

Taking Care of Pigeons

When I went to Colgate on my recruiting visit, the coach had showed me the architectural drawings of the proposed field house. This plan included the construction of an indoor track that certainly would've resolved many of the practice issues that my teammates and I encountered in our four years as undergraduates. The year after I left Colgate for Bucknell was when the indoor facility was finally constructed—only six years after my recruiting visit. As with the majority of buildings on the campus, the field house was built with a stone façade and a slate roof. While the building was going up, several families of pigeons had nested in the rafters inside the building. After the roof was in place and the walls were all up, the flooring company came in to lay down the track surface and the artificial turf for the infield.

When the floor company arrived, they refused to lay down the floor until the bird problem was resolved, for they didn't believe the track surface would adhere to the base with the quantity of bird crap on the floor. The contractors tried everything to get rid of the birds: leaving the lights on all night, high-pitched noises, and loud bangs—anything to encourage the birds to leave the building, but nothing worked.

Finally, a local farmer heard about the dilemma and volunteered to take care of the problem, as he claimed he'd had the same pigeon problem in his barn the previous year and had a solution. Without anyone from the contractor's firm or the school present, the farmer came into the field house early one Saturday morning and got rid of all the pigeons. He did indeed take care of the problem and it wasn't until the next time it rained that it occurred to anyone as to how he'd accomplished what no one else was able to do. The brand-new slate roof had the exact same number of holes in it as there had been pigeons in the building. The farmer had come in with a gun and shot all the birds, naturally putting holes in the brand-new roof at the same time. The school had to replace numerous pieces of slate, but at least the floor got laid down.

The Internet?

I worked at a school at one point that had a snack bar in the athletic building to serve various items for people in a hurry after working out. The school came up with a catchy name for the snack bar that was appropriate for an athletic venue and celebrated the grand opening in style. The student body was very fond of the facility and the snack bar became quite a successful venture for the food services company at the school.

Amazingly enough, a restaurant in Florida had an identical name as the snack bar in our athletic facility. Somehow, the Florida establishment—more than 1,200 miles away—discovered that our school was using the same name for our campus snack bar as their restaurant. The supposition was that someone figured it out by doing a search on the Internet.

The restaurant's attorney contacted the school and informed them that the school had to terminate the use of the name, as the restaurant owned the rights and the school was infringing on the restaurant's rights. Give me a break. Did that restaurant really think that a school more than 1,000 miles away was somehow going to hurt its business and steal away potential customers?

The school did end up taking the name down and renamed the snack bar, but what's the big deal? To me, this was a classic example of rights superseding common sense. There was absolutely no reason for the restaurant to require the school to do this and it was utterly ridiculous to threaten the school with a lawsuit to protect its name.

It's a Tunnel

We used to go to an indoor meet at the University of Rochester every year when I was in college. Rochester has the most unique indoor track I've ever seen. The building was constructed quite a long time ago and every attempt was made to maximize space.

The basketball court was built with permanent immovable bleachers on either sideline. On the other side of the wall behind one basket was an auxiliary gym with Astroturf on the floor for spring sports to use during the rather harsh winters. Around the perimeter of the auxiliary gym was a four-lane track, although the total distance of the track within this space was only 100 meters. In order to construct a track of the proper 200 meters in length, a hole was cut out of the cinder blocks on the wall dividing the basketball court to the auxiliary gym. The track was then extended underneath the permanent bleachers of the basketball court to finish off the 200-meter oval.

So, if I've not done a good enough job of explaining this, half of the track encircled the auxiliary gym and the other half of the track surrounded the basketball court underneath the bleachers of the basketball court. Therefore, half of the track was a tunnel. If that wasn't unique enough, the really crazy part of the facility was that there were four lanes going into the tunnel but only three lanes coming out of the tunnel. All track races are run counterclockwise and this track could handle four coming in but only three going out.

This made for some rather interesting races from an athlete's perspective as well from as a spectator's perspective. I can't tell you how many times the person that went into the tunnel with the lead didn't come out with the lead and sometimes just flat out didn't come out of the tunnel. Pushing and shoving were the norm in there, and every once in a while, a bloody athlete would return with horror stories about running or being run into a wall. Track isn't supposed to be a contact sport, but the University of Rochester's indoor track mandates that it become one.

Turn Off the Soda Machine

I served as the USA Track & Field national triple jump chairman for the men's development committee for six years and subsequently served as the overall chairman of the development committee for seven years. During that time, I had many wonderful experiences and was afforded the opportunity to travel all over the country and, on a few occasions, to Europe and South America serving in this capacity.

One of the most beautiful places I was able to travel to very frequently was the ARCO Olympic Training Center in Chula Vista, California. Chula Vista is south of San Diego and borders Mexico—just north of Tijuana. The training center is spectacular and serves as the Olympic training center for track and field, soccer, softball, archery, tennis, and crew—to name a few. The sports facilities are spectacular and the track facility is the best I've ever seen.

The entire center is very picturesque, as it sits right on a reservoir and is nestled in the some foothills in Southern California. Every time I've visited the center, I can feel the weight come right off my shoulders and I'm immediately in awe of the surroundings. It's really a beautiful place.

The archery venue sits on top of a hill, with a wonderful view of the reservoir in one direction and Tijuana in the other direction. The venue also has a small building with restrooms, storage areas, and a soda machine. Without thinking anything of it, the planners of the facility built this building in such a manner that the soda machine faces south—or toward Mexico.

The U.S. Border Patrol ultimately had to ask the management of the training center to turn the soda machine off at night, as they discovered that people trying to get across the border used the light of the machine as a beacon for their escape over the border. The border patrol had learned through a series of interrogations of people whom they'd caught trying to cross the border that it was common knowledge in Mexico that if you made it to the soda machine, you had safely crossed the border. Bet you never heard that one before.

Soccer Stadium and a Slaughterhouse

At one point in my career, I was working at a school that had decided to build a new soccer venue. The school owned a rather large piece of property adjacent to the rest of the athletic facilities and the decision was made to relocate the soccer stadium to have it included in the athletic department's complex.

The piece of property that the school intended to put the soccer stadium on was a slopping hill next to an existing parking lot within the athletic facility and the only problem with the property was that one building needed to be removed for the stadium to be built.

The trucks came in one morning with the intent of leveling the slope, flattening out the property, and tearing down the building. The initial demolition and leveling of the field was only scheduled to last a couple days. The soccer coach at the time happened to be out in his yard after work the day the demolition had begun and was paid a visit by his elderly next-door neighbor.

"I happened to drive by your office today and noticed the destruction of the building on the corner. What are you guys planning on doing over there?" the neighbor inquired.

"We're finally building that soccer field I've been asking for. Why do you ask?" was our soccer coach's response.

The neighbor gave our soccer coach the following information: "When I was a little kid back before World War II, that building was a slaughterhouse. I'm pretty sure I remember that they buried two 500-gallon tanks below the building and that those tanks were used to store the blood and guts when they butchered the animals."

Of course, the next day, our soccer coach went in and told the athletic director that story he'd heard the night before regarding the slaughterhouse and the storage tanks. "No," the athletic director said, "we've had city planners, engineers, and construction experts all over this site for months. The story this guy told you last night just isn't true."

As soon as the athletic director told the coach that the tanks don't exist, the foreman of the job walked in and told the athletic director: "We've got a problem out on the field. Our bulldozer just struck some kind of tank underneath the building that we tore down and some kind of liquid is oozing out all over the field we just leveled."

The EPA ended up having to be called in, and after an extensive analysis of the area, they determined that the liquid from the tanks was toxic and that all the dirt that the liquid had seeped into must be removed before construction could continue.

I don't remember how many dump trucks' worth of dirt ended up being removed nor do I remember the exact amount of the cost the school incurred to have the toxic dirt removed, but I do remember that the cost for removal far exceeded the initial cost estimates for the entire project. Thousands and thousands of dollars could have been saved if someone had at least listened to our soccer coach's next-door neighbor.

We Need New Turf

I wrote at the beginning of this chapter that Murphy's Law oftentimes rears its ugly head in athletics. I'll conclude by writing one more classic definition of this law.

A few years back, I was working at a school that needed to replace the Astroturf on the football field. Contracts were signed, plans made, and a timetable established in order to have the job done entirely during summer vacation so it wouldn't affect any practice schedules.

The week after the school year ended, a group came in and removed the old turf. It went without a hitch and the next stage of the project was ready to start on schedule. That stage was to include the installation of a layer of crushed stone and to have that layer rolled with a steamroller in preparation for the installation of the e-layer—the layer that goes on directly below the turf itself.

After the stone had been rolled, the e-layer company came in and right away told the contractor there had been two mistakes made in the installation of the crushed stone and that the company wouldn't put the e-layer down until the mistakes had been corrected. The first was that the size of the stones weren't up to their specifications and the weight of the steamroller hadn't been calibrated correctly. Therefore, the stones were too solidly encased, which would prevent water draining correctly below the field.

The only solution was to remove all the crushed stone that had been in place and start over again. The subcontractor in charge of this facet of the project begrudgingly returned with his crew and proceeded to begin the arduous process of removing recently crushed stone on an entire football field. While in the process of doing this, the company ripped several of the drains underneath this layer of the field. The project stopped in its tracks, as the school wasn't going to allow the project to continue until the drains had been repaired satisfactorily. This took several weeks, as experts on football field drains don't live in every town and one would have to think that the time demands on people with this area of expertise is quite extensive during the summer months.

Finally, a drain expert was available and the drainage system was repaired. Five to six weeks after the initial layer of incorrect stone was installed, the proper stones were installed and rolled to the proper specifications. Murphy's Law then reared its head again. The contractor had placed plywood over the track to protect it all summer when the construction vehicles were driving over it onto the football field. Just when the stone was completed and ready for the e-layer installations, a construction worker drove his pickup truck over the track onto the football field and a piece of the plywood somehow popped up and punctured a hole in his gas tank, causing him to leak an entire tankful of gas onto the newly deposited stone.

Obviously, the e-layer once again had to be delayed, as all the affected stone from the spilled gasoline had to be removed, as it was deemed toxic. This took another week, then the stone had to be redone, and, finally, the e-layer was poured. Once that facet was completed, the turf company could finally come in to install the final product—only about eight weeks behind schedule.

The project finally was completed the day before the first home contest of the year, so one could argue that all's well that ends well, but it did force all the fall sports that use the facility to scramble during preseason training camps for alternative sights to practice.

Everything that can go wrong does go wrong!

12

Camps, Clinics, and T-Shirts: Any Way to Make an Extra Buck

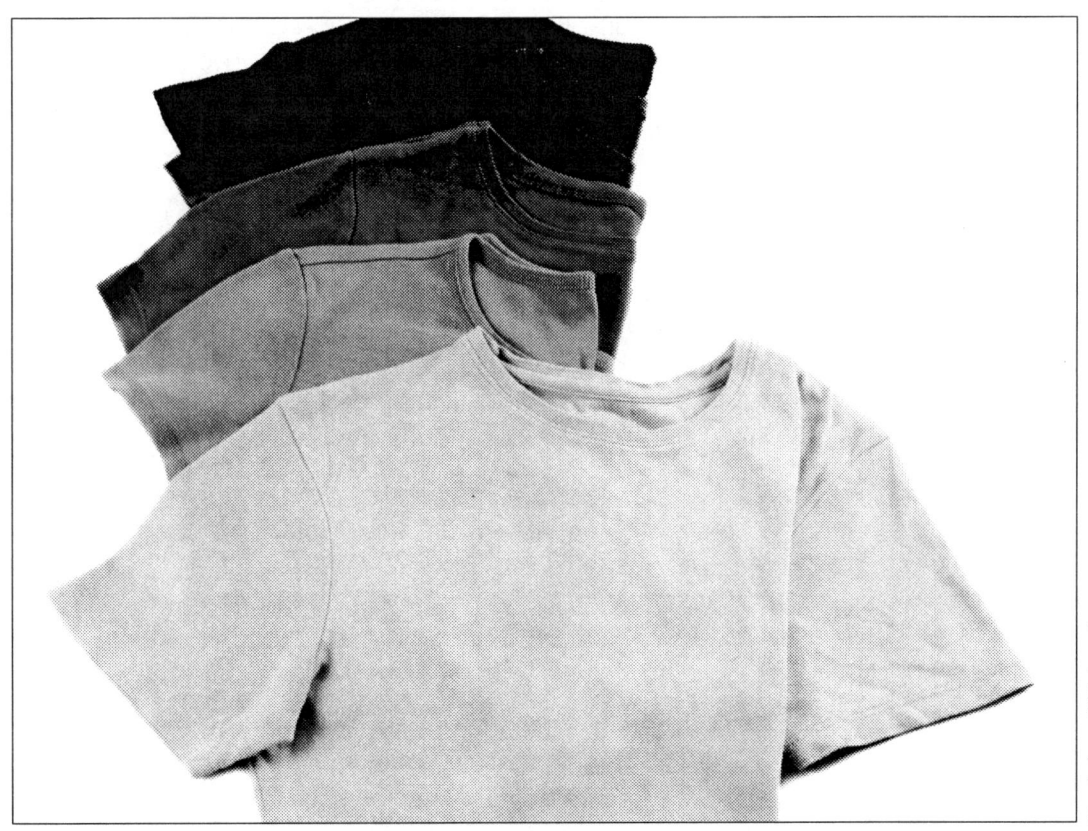

Close to the end of my coaching tenure at Syracuse, the local newspaper listed the average salary of the head coaches and the full-time assistant coaches in our department. The paper didn't single out any coach nor did it single out any specific sport. It just listed the average salary of the coaches in the department. At any level of college athletics, especially at the Division I level, the head football and basketball coaches make a significantly greater amount of money than the other coaches in the department. One can also make a safe assumption that the assistant coaches in those two sports not only make more money than the assistant coaches in the other sports, but in all likelihood, they earn more than the head coaches in the nonrevenue sports.

The newspaper article didn't do a very good job of differentiating this rather important fact in their article, as there was a definitive insinuation in the article that all the coaches in the department were making the kind of money listed in the article. There were, though, a significant number of coaches, including myself, that weren't even close to the numbers listed in the newspaper article.

When I lived in Syracuse, I owned small home in a rather modest neighborhood, and upon learning I coached in the athletic department, my next-door neighbor got into the habit of waiting outside around the time I arrived home from work each day in order to pepper me with questions regarding the latest gossip in our department. Needless to say, the evening after the local paper had listed the average salary, there was my next-door neighbor waiting for me at the end of my driveway when I arrived home from work. "What are you doing living in this neighborhood?" he inquired. "I read in the paper this morning what you.re earning. You certainly can afford a house in a better neighborhood than this one."

I tried to explain to him that the 10 assistant football coaches and two men's and two women's assistant basketball coaches all earned significantly more than I did as an assistant track coach. Or, for that matter, more than the assistant soccer, swimming, field hockey, or volleyball assistants too. He absolutely wanted no part of my explanation and said as he walked away, "I know what I read in today's paper."

I bring this story up because people have frequent misconceptions regarding the salaries coaches earn. I've never met a coach who started out in this career because of the money. Coaches get into the business for three reasons: their love of their chosen sport, their desire to continue to be in a competitive environment, and their commitment to use their sport to teach and help young adults. It has nothing to do with money.

With that said, though, a coach still needs to earn enough money to support himself, and oftentimes, young coaches will do almost anything to earn extra money. I mentioned earlier in the book that during my first couple years in coaching, I checked IDs at fraternity parties, worked as a substitute teacher, painted houses, and worked in the admission office to earn enough money to coach. As the years have passed, more and more opportunities to earn extra money have presented themselves. Coaching at camps, speaking at track clinics, and even selling T-shirts at track meets are just a few of the things I've done along the way to make enough money to pursue my dream of being a college coach.

T-Shirts for Sale

Early on in my tenure at Syracuse, I served as the meet director for the Division I Women's Indoor ECAC Championship. The ECAC Championship is comprised of nearly every Division I school in the geographic area from Maine to Virginia. At the time, more than 120 Division I schools were within this region. To this day, the ECAC Indoor Championship falls the weekend before the NCAA Championship and therefore is the last opportunity athletes have to qualify for indoor nationals. Teams take the meet very seriously and at least 500 participants compete.

I made the decision to make a few extra dollars by ordering a gross (144) of T-shirts, designing a logo for the meet, having the logo silk-screened on the shirts, and selling them at the meet. This is quite common at many larger meets and I was quite confident I was going to sell all the shirts for $15 a shirt.

The meet was a two-day competition, and after the first day, I'd successfully sold more than half the shirts, so I was sure I'd be able to sell the rest of the shirts the second day. About halfway through the second day, I went over to the student I had hired to sell the shirts to inquire as to how many shirts were left and I found out we still had at least 25 shirts left. I had no desire to have leftover shirts, so I decided to cut the price down to $10 per shirt.

Track and field is divided into two primary event areas: field events and track events. Track events consist of all the running events, including the hurdles. Field events are divided into two areas: throwing events (shot put, discus, javelin, and the hammer throw) and jumping events (long jump, triple jump, high jump, and pole vault). In the field events, the athletes compete in a predetermined order. The official in each of these events will always call off three names after each attempt. The athlete who's to compete next in the order is called first and the official will announce the individual's last name as "up" and then announce the next name as "on deck" and the person who's third in the order as "in the hole." So, it will often sound something like "Jones up, Smith on deck, Jackson in the hole." This way, the athlete has a very good idea as to when they're next going to make an attempt. Once an individual is announced as "up," he or she has 60 seconds to make an attempt.

After I decided to discount the price of the shirts, I went over to our announcer and told her to announce over the loudspeaker that the T-shirts were now being discounted to $10 on a first-come, first-serve basis. The finals of the triple jump were going on at the time of the announcement and the athlete who was in third place going into the final round of attempts was on the runway, having already been called "up" when the announcement of the discount was made.

I was once fortunate enough to be at the USA National Championships when the world record in the men's 100-meter dash was broken. When the announcement was made for discounted shirts, the woman on the triple jump runway moved faster than the athletes in that 100-meter dash. In one smooth and continuous movement, she grabbed her bag, which was sitting next to the runway, sprinted the 20 yards to where the shirts were being sold, threw a $10 bill on the table, grabbed a shirt, and was back on the runway within her allotted 60 seconds. To make it even more impressive, she then proceeded to run down the runway and jumped far enough to put herself into first place and qualify for the NCAA Championship. All in 60 seconds. Amazing.

The postscript to the story is that a couple days after the meet, I had a coach with at least 20 years of coaching experience call me up and tell me that several of his kids who'd bought shirts the first day for the $15 price wanted a $5 refund because I had dropped the price the second day. "Coach," I said, "you've been at college track meets for at least as long as I have and I know of at least six meets a year that both your team and my team compete where the same thing is done. If your kids wanted to save that $5, they certainly could have risked waiting to buy a shirt the second day." I stopped selling T-shirts after that.

Clinics

Another way to make some extra money is to host track clinics or to speak at clinics hosted by other schools or organizations. Over the years, I've had the opportunity to speak at many clinics in at least 30 different states and have hosted at least six or eight clinics myself.

Essentially, two different kinds of clinics exist: learn-by-doing clinics and lecture hall–style clinics. In a learn-by-doing environment, the attendees are encouraged to dress in workout clothing and are expected to participate in the clinic by actually performing the various drills being demonstrated by the speakers, whereas a lecture clinic is quite self-explanatory: The speaker stands up at a lectern and the attendees sit and take notes.

I used to enjoy hosting clinics until one year I learned my lesson. It had never occurred to me to put in writing on the clinic brochure that the clinic would go on no matter what the weather conditions. Proving the theory that you're never a profit in your own hometown, the annual clinic I hosted in Syracuse drew people from more than 200 miles away but rarely had anyone from within 10 miles. The second or third year of the clinic, we experienced a monster of a snowstorm the night before the clinic. I probably had between 250 and 300 people preregistered for the clinic and almost none of them attended the clinic. I ended up reimbursing all the preregistration fees because I hadn't stipulated in the brochure "rain or shine." Snow in Syracuse—who'd have ever guessed?

Somewhere along the way, I received some very sound advice from a rather experienced person in the world of track and field with regard to speaking at clinics. He told me that most people who attend clinics don't want to go home thinking they don't know anything and that they need to change the entire way they coach. They want to go home from a clinic thinking they learned some new ideas and concepts but that for the most part, they're doing a good job within their own program. "So," he went on, "don't try to prove to all the people attending one of your sessions how much you know, but teach them some basic concepts, be enthusiastic, and really show the audience you're working hard and trying to teach them."

I took this advice to heart and since then have always believed that an audience will really enjoy my presentation if I work hard, sweat a lot, and show them I'm very enthusiastic about the topic I'm speaking about. Over the years, this advice has served me quite well, but it has also gotten me into some trouble over the years.

During the 1996 Olympic Trials in Atlanta, USA Track & Field hosted a clinic in conjunction with the meet. I was giving a talk on the long jump in a classroom of a local high school and was running up and down the center aisle of the classroom demonstrating various long jump drills. At some point during the lecture, I made the decision I didn't have enough room to demonstrate a particular drill within the confines of the classroom but determined that I did have enough room to demonstrate the drill if I finished by exiting the door leading out into the hallway. I was grossly mistaken by the estimation of how much room I needed to demonstrate the drill and ended up hitting my head on the top of the doorframe as I was exiting the classroom at full speed. I nearly knocked myself out and put a pretty good gash in my forehead, but I continued with the lecture.

Another time, I was speaking at a clinic in Atlantic City, New Jersey, at a clinic with about 1,200 people in attendance. I was giving my lecture in a rather large ballroom, so I ended up standing on top of a table in order for the people in the back of the room to be able to see me. At one point, I clearly forgot I was standing on a table and demonstrated some kind of jumping drill in which I jumped straight up vertically. I put my head right through a ceiling tile and once again continued on with the lecture as if nothing had happened. I'm absolutely willing to sacrifice my body for the audience!

Years ago, I was speaking at a clinic at a college in Boston and the coach had reserved a biology lecture hall for the clinic. I was in the middle of a talk on the triple jump, demonstrating drill after drill and sweating like a pig. I was demonstrating all the drills on top of a lab table as once again I wanted the people in the back to be able to see what I was demonstrating. I was in the middle of demonstrating a particular exercise when a member of the audience started waving her hand as if she wanted to ask a question. Because I was in the middle of something and didn't want to lose my train of thought, I continued on, thinking I'd call on her after I was done with the particular drill. She persisted in waving her hands and I continued to avoid her until she finally couldn't take it anymore and screamed out: "You kicked the gas line on. You better stop and turn it off before it catches on fire!" Of course, I immediately stopped and turned off the gas, as it's one thing to sacrifice myself for the audience, but it's another thing entirely to sacrifice the audience.

Camps

As with clinics, various kinds of track camps also exist. Camps that are run on college campuses are usually private enterprises run by the head coach of a particular sport at the school. The coach runs the camp as a moneymaking venture and usually has to pay some kind of usage fee back to the school in general or the athletic department specifically. USA Track & Field, the governing body of the sport in our country, also has a variety of camps. These camps are usually either an elite-level training camp for athletes ranked in the top 5 to 10 in their event in the country or junior elite camps, which are for the top athletes under the age of 19. The junior elite and elite camps are usually held at an Olympic training center.

I have experience at all three aforementioned levels of camps and have to say that both levels of camps geared toward youth—the private camps and the junior elite camps—have supplied me with a bevy of stories.

I Smell Beer

When I coached at Bucknell, the head coach had an extraordinarily successful set of summer track and cross-country camps. He hosted back-to-back weeks of camps in mid-August: The first week was a track and field camp and the second week was a cross-country camp. Each camp had in the neighborhood of 150 to 200 high school campers and in the range of 10 to 15 coaches and counselors. Because I was a member of the Bucknell coaching staff, one of my responsibilities during these two weeks of camp was to make sure the kids were in their rooms at night after the evening session and were in their beds with their lights turned off at the designated time.

Somewhere in the middle of the second week, after having served as a sentry for eight or nine nights in a row, I was beginning to get a little frustrated that I had to walk the halls and the exterior of the dorm while some of the other coaches were down at a local watering hole enjoying their free time. As I roamed the space outside the dorm feeling sorry for myself, I thought I was experiencing a mirage as I smelled beer. "I shouldn't be smelling beer right now," I thought. "My imagination must be playing tricks on me."

The sensation persisted as I continued my walk around the building and I also began to hear a great deal of laughter coming from one of the rooms on the second floor. Inside I went, up the stairs I jogged, and down the hall I continued until I came to the room where I heard laughter. Using the master key I'd been given as the night's sentry, I was shocked at what I saw inside the room. There sat six to eight guys from the same New Jersey high school, a refrigerator in the corner, and seven or eight cases of beer under the beds and another case or two inside the refrigerator. These kids had really come to this camp ready to party.

I went downstairs to the head coach's room and brought him back upstairs to the kids' room. We ended up confiscating more than nine cases of beer—great for me in one respect as a young coach not making much money, as I wasn't going to have to buy any beer that upcoming school year.

The head coach immediately told the kids to pack their bags and report to the lobby of the dorm in 10 minutes. He then called each one of their parents, told them what had happened, and requested they come that night and pick up their children. All the parents complied and the kids were all gone within a few hours of the discovery of their party room.

The story didn't end there, though, as, remarkably, a few days later, the kids' high school coach called our head coach and really chewed him out. "How dare you kick my kids out of camp. You had no right to do that," he explained. "We have a great chance of winning the state championship this fall and I was planning on using your camp to get the kids in shape. Now it's going to be much more difficult for us to win the championship." Our head coach responded by asking, "You mean to tell me you're more concerned about the state championship than you are with the fact that eight members of your team—all of whom are underage—were drinking?"

The high school coach really didn't respond to the question but made a threat instead: "I'll never send anyone to your camp again!" I don't know what amazed me more—the kids having the audacity to bring nine cases of beer to a cross-country camp or their high school coach responding the way he did. He may never have sent his kids to that camp again, but it's been more than 20 years since that incident and never again have I recruited an athlete from that high school.

Never Trust a High School Pole Vaulter You Don't Know

For seven years, I served as the chairman of the men's development committee for USA Track & Field. The position meant I was in charge of a $400,000 annual budget and a committee of about 20 people. The committee members were responsible for a variety of things. Some were the chairman of a particular event, such as the long jump or the high hurdles, while others were regional chairs or the national junior elite camp chair. Because I was the overall chair of the committee, my responsibilities consisted of chairing our annual meeting, attending various event-specific summits and camps, and serving as the liaison between the men's and women's development committees, the sports science committee, and the athlete advisory committee.

I also attended the annual national junior elite summer camp, which was held at the Olympic Training Center in Chula Vista, California. The training center is a beautiful facility and it serves as the training site for track and field, softball, tennis, soccer, and crew—to name a few of the Olympic sports that use this particular facility.

The camp lasted four days and most of the event-specific national chairs attended the camp, as the instructors and the top 5 to 10 high school athletes in the nation in each event were invited to the camp. It was a marvelous opportunity for the athletes and it also afforded the event chairs to get to know the rising stars in the event area they were responsible for.

One year, I chose to stay in San Diego the night after the camp ended and fly home the following day. Because the camp had ended, I stayed in a very nice hotel in downtown San Diego across the street from the airport. Several of the other coaches and athletes were in similar situations and a couple the athletes who'd attended the camp slept on the floor of the room I was sharing with one of the other coaches.

One of the kids staying on the floor was a pole vaulter from somewhere in the Midwest who'd already committed to attend college in Southern California the following semester and had actually utilized the camp as his means of traveling out to California from home in preparation for his first college semester. He'd told people during the week of the camp that he'd already made arrangements with his future college coach for the coach to come down and pick him up at the end of camp and bring him back to his new school.

The coach I was sharing the room with and I had very early morning flights back to the East Coast and the athlete assured us that when we got up in the morning to go to the airport that he'd also get up and head down to the lobby of the hotel and wait for his new coach to come pick him up. When morning came and the other coach and I were getting ready to leave, the athlete told us he'd called his college coach and he'd not be able to arrive at the hotel until around 11 a.m. and because it was only 6 a.m., would we mind if he stayed in bed until checkout time at 10:30? Seemed harmless enough to me and, sadly, because the room was on my credit card, I wasn't at all skeptical of his story.

I didn't give it another thought, left for the airport, and didn't think about it again until three weeks later when my credit card bill arrived. He had totally cleaned out the honor bar and drank and eaten more than $300 worth of beer, wine, soda, and food and left me with the bill. Of course, I called the coach at the college he was supposed to attend and the coach confirmed that, yes, the athlete had intended to attend his college, but he'd never shown up and the coach had never heard from him again. I learned years later that he'd hitchhiked across the country to the Midwest, never went to college, and never competed in the pole vault again either.

Lake Placid Training Camp

Early on in my coaching career, the men's and women's development committees for USA Track & Field had regional chairpersons. These chairs were essentially responsible for hosting an annual regional junior elite camp. The eastern regional camp for a couple years in the early 1980s was hosted at the Olympic Training Center in Lake Placid, New

York. Although the majority of the facilities at this particular training center were geared toward winter sports, we were able to have the camp there and use the outdoor track at one of the local high schools.

For two or three years in a row, I was fortunate enough to be asked to work with the high jumpers at this camp. One year at this camp, the high school boys were put on the first two floors of the dormitory and the high school girls were placed on the top two floors of the same dorm. At the beginning of the week, the director of the boys' camp and the girls' camp read them the riot act and explained that no boys were going to be allowed on the girls' floors and vice versa. The kids were told that if they disobeyed this rule, they'd be sent home from the camp.

The dormitory was a standard four-story building with a brick façade and each room was a typical dorm room with two beds, two dressers, and two closets. Nothing fancy, but it certainly sufficed and served its purpose of housing athletes. One night, several of the coaches had walked down the road to a local bar named—I kid you not—the City Dump. As we approached the dorm on our way back, one of the male jumpers who was staying on the second floor was scaling the outside wall of the dorm trying to make it up to the girls' floor. He was using the mortar gaps between each row of bricks as finger and toe holds and he appeared like Spider-Man as he made his way up the face of the building.

We determined we were better off staying quiet and letting him reach the next floor rather than scare him in midclimb, but as soon as he'd safely made it up to the third floor, we ran up the stairs and pulled him out of the girl's room he'd just climbed into to and brought him back to the boys' floor. Crazy, of course, but you have to admit rather an athletic maneuver.

One year, during the last night of the camp, the male campers decided to have a water fight outside in the parking lot. The kids were throwing water balloons at each other and dumping water on each other's heads when, unfortunately, one of the athletes filled a glass Gatorade® bottle up with water, and as he went to throw water on one of the other campers, the bottle slipped out of his wet hands and the bottle smashed on the face of one of the athletes. I spent the night with him in the emergency room and he ended up being fine but had to get several stitches in his forehead. It always makes for a tough drive home when you've been up all night babysitting a high school kid in the hospital who got hurt doing something as stupid as a water fight.

Anyway, back to more interesting stories that took place at the training center in Lake Placid. At one point during the mid-1980s, USA Bobsled made a decision that it should recruit former track athletes to push the bobsleds. The organization was essentially looking for fast, powerful former collegiate athletes to be pushers for their team. USA Bobsled is based in Lake Placid and the president of its association invited all the coaches at our camp to a social one evening in order to explain its objective and to encourage us to suggest this for our graduating athletes who weren't pursuing track after college.

One of the members of the federation owned a bar in the little village of Lake Placid and the social was held at his establishment. The members of the association went through an entire presentation for us as to what kind of athletes they were looking for, how they proposed we could assist them, what they could do for us, etc. It was a very impressive presentation and I'm sure several coaches already had in mind some of their graduating athletes for this program.

After the presentation, they told us they wanted to show us a 20-minute highlight video of USA Bobsled. It was rather exciting to watch the video, especially because several of the drivers and pushers—past and present—were sitting in the bar with us and were adding their thoughts and insights as we continued to watch the sleds storm down the various bobsled runs throughout the world. At one point during the video, a rather horrific crash of a U.S. bobsled occurred. Several guys sitting in the room bowed their heads while others patted one of the other people sitting in the room on the back and gave him rather sympathetic glances.

Come to find out that his brother had actually been killed in the accident we'd just watched on the screen. I'll never forget that. Here we were sitting in a room being encouraged by a group of guys to suggest to our former athletes why they should pursue bobsledding after they graduated from college and one of the guys sitting in the room suggesting this to us had actually lost a family member participating in the sport they were suggesting we get involved with. Now that's dedication to a sport.

13

The Blizzard of 1993 ... and the Roof That Came Down

In 1990, Syracuse University and the Syracuse track and field coaching staff began serving as the host for the High School National Indoor Track and Field Championships. The track staff's responsibilities were kept to a minimum, as the Metropolitan Athletics Congress (MAC—the New York City area association for USA Track & Field—was actually in charge of the meet. Thus, all the Syracuse coaching staff had to do was ensure that the facility was properly set up and the MAC would take care of the rest.

The Carrier Dome annually served as the site for this grand competition—a meet that consisted of 1,600 high school athletes from all 50 states. Oftentimes, a high school athlete walking into the Carrier Dome for the first time would be totally awestruck by the imposing structure of the dome. Although the Carrier Dome no longer has an indoor track underneath the football field, back then, the track in the dome was second to none. It had an eight-lane oval—which was quite rare for an indoor track, as most indoor facilities are normally only large enough for a six-lane track—wonderful spread-out field event venues, and 50,000 seats. Unfortunately, in this day and age of Americans being in favor of instant gratification and therefore only identifying with high-scoring, fast-paced sports, the majority of those 50,000 seats were always empty even for a meet as high caliber as a national championship. The MAC always dressed up the facility very well for the function, with flags from all 50 states, banners throughout the building, and even a giant blowup Foot Locker doll.

The meet had always run smoothly until 1993, when the event happened to fall on the same weekend as the greatest blizzard to hit the East Coast in the 20th century. The meet was always scheduled for a two-day competition, and for this particular year, it was Saturday and Sunday, March 13 and 14. Saturday morning began as scheduled with the boys' and girls' pentathlons, an event composed of the hurdles, long jump, shot put, high jump, and either the 1,000-meter run for boys or the 800-meter run for girls. The competition started at 10 a.m., and by noon, it was becoming apparent that we were in for a long weekend. The snow began to fall by 8 a.m., and at 2:30 p.m., we had to make an announcement that the remainder of Saturday's competition would have to be postponed due to a growing concern over the snow. This decision was based on the athletes' safety in returning to their hotels and more importantly—although certainly not announced to the crowd—the growing concern about the weight of the snow on the roof.

The Carrier Dome's roof weighs 200 tons and consists of 287,000 square feet of Teflon®-coated fiberglass and 14 three-inch-thick steel bridge cables. Sixteen five-foot-diameter fans provide air pressure to keep the roof up. Under normal winter conditions, the temperature inside the building is raised, enabling the snow to melt off the roof. Only once prior to the 1993 blizzard had the roof been lowered due to excessive weight on the roof and this was because of a severe ice storm several years earlier.

As the snow continued to fall through the late morning and early afternoon, the safe and prudent thing to do was to send the 1,600 athletes back to their hotels to wait out the storm. At the time, no one—including me—had any idea as to the length of time that the athletes would ultimately have to endure before setting foot back on a track to conclude the competition.

After the athletes departed the dome, the manager of the facility, the meet director, and I sat for quite some time to discuss any and all options we had to try to finish the meet. Naturally, the remainder of Saturday was out of the question, and as the weather reports continued to become worse rather than better, Sunday was beginning to also appear bleak.

The university's athletic department did have another indoor track in Manley Field House—otherwise known to old-time college basketball fans as the Zoo because the Syracuse men's basketball team had once won 57 straight games in Manley. The Orange basketball team ended its winning streak in Manley by losing the very last game ever played there before moving to the Carrier Dome. Eric "Sleepy" Floyd of Georgetown hit two free throws with five seconds left to propel Georgetown to victory and after the game Hoyas coach John Thompson stated: "Manley Field House is officially closed."

The field house may have been closed for men's basketball games back in 1980, but it still served as the track team's home base and was a wonderful facility for track meets. After several hours of discussing our options for the continuation of the meet, it appeared that the dome would be incapacitated and the only chance we had of finishing the meet was to move the competition to Manley. So, as I departed the dome on Saturday in the early evening, I thought the track equipment would begin to be moved to the field house and I assumed we'd be starting up again in Manley first thing Sunday morning. As soon as I walked outside to my car, I knew I was wrong, as we'd already gotten at least 2.5 feet of snow and the forecasters were claiming at that point that the storm wasn't even half over yet.

Fighting my way home the four miles from the dome to my house through an ever-increasing amount of snow, I began to wonder if we were totally unrealistic to think we had a shot in the world of ever finishing the meet. An hour after leaving campus, I finally arrived home after getting stuck in snow drifts on several different occasions. Upon arriving home after such a difficult and frustrating drive, I assumed I wouldn't leave my home again until the end of the storm. Boy was I wrong.

As soon as I arrived home, the phone began to ring. High school coaches calling wanting to know what the status of the meet was in order to relay information to their frustrated athletes, college coaches stuck in airports en route to Syracuse wanting to know if they should continue on in their futile attempts to arrive at the meet in order to recruit and, of course, the Carrier Dome manager and the meet director calling in updates on the future plans of the meet. Sometime during Saturday evening—in between rather worthless attempts to keep my driveway clean—I learned that the power in Manley Field House was out, as the building's transformer had blown due to excess snow, rendering the field house powerless. Clearly, at this point, the meet being run on Sunday was out of the question.

Two items on the 11 p.m. news that Saturday night came across the screen that surely indicated the meet was never to be finished. The university had announced that the school was not only officially closed on Sunday, but it had already made the decision to not be open on Monday either. We happened to be coming to the end of our spring break that weekend and university officials had logically determined they didn't want 10,000 students making an attempt to return to Syracuse on Sunday afternoon and thought that the weather would allow for a safe return on Monday afternoon instead, thus cancelling classes on Monday. The other upsetting report was the weather report itself, as the local forecasters were now predicting at least 45 inches of snow by the end of the storm. With the updated weather report, the mayor decided in a rather unusual act for a city in the snow belt to declare a state of emergency.

What a state of emergency meant was that the snowplows were called in off the streets and wouldn't return to remove snow until after the storm had stopped. No one was allowed out on the streets and no snow would be removed until the end of the storm. Clearly an end to the potential of hosting a high school track meet, but I didn't know at this point who I was dealing with in the always-thinking and somewhat magical meet director from the MAC.

Finally having fallen asleep at 1 am on Sunday morning, I knew I was going to have to wake up by 4:45 a.m., as we'd planned on a 5 a.m. conference call with all the key players to discuss the status of the Carrier Dome and our various options for the continuation of the meet. As dawn arrived and the conference call concluded, it was quite apparent that not only was the dome not available for the meet, but it was out of commission. When the weight on the roof became too excessive, the only way to prevent the roof from caving in on itself was to actually take the air out of the dome and deflate the roof. As the surface area inside the dome decreased, the heat was turned up and the snow slowly but surely melted off the roof. During the course of Saturday night, the decision had been made—with all the track equipment still on the floor of the facility—to let the roof down. Not only did I learn that the dome was deflated, but I was also told that the power in the field house was still out. Again, I concluded that the meet was therefore going to have to be cancelled permanently, but for the second or third time, I was grossly mistaken.

Go back to sleep? Certainly not. By 5:45 a.m., the phone began to ring almost continuously. The wheels of the organizing committee had started to turn as it was developing options to contest the meet, which I found almost impossible to believe. The questions I was being asked seemed totally irrelevant for the running of a track meet. "Where's the university's chancellor? How close is the nearest National Guard? How many trucks can you locate over the next several hours?" I not so politely in my sleep-deprived state informed these inquisitive minds that I didn't know what it was like at the schools where they worked, but here at Syracuse, the chancellor normally didn't inform an assistant track coach as to his every move and my response to their early morning questions seemed quite logical to me: "How the hell should I know?"

By 11 a.m., Sunday morning, with the snow still falling at an incredible rate, the meet director called me again with an odd and seemingly impossible plan. As it happened to be, the High School Indoor National Track and Field Championships' meet director was also the son of the Rhode Island governor, so the governor of Rhode Island had called Mario Cuomo, New York's governor, and convinced New York State's leader that despite this horrific storm, despite the state of emergency, and despite the fact that the university was already officially closed that every effort must be made to run this track meet. Incredibly enough, Cuomo agreed and promised to send the National Guard to help me make plans to continue to host this meet no matter what.

In my humble and, at this point, rather inconsequential opinion, we still had some rather obvious stumbling blocks to overcome. The meet director may have had the governor's approval, but Syracuse is a private school with no direct reporting requirements to the governor and the school was still officially closed. The next call I received from the meet director was again the same question as the previous call: "Where's the chancellor?" Again, as with the first time I was confronted with this rather unusual question, I reiterated that historically our chancellor didn't see the need in keeping me abreast to his daily routine and I had no idea what was on his itinerary for that particular Sunday morning. Miraculously, the meet director eventually tracked down the chancellor. That weekend also happened to be when the annual Big East basketball tournament in Madison Square Garden took place and Syracuse was in the finals. The meet director paged the chancellor at MSG, got him on the phone, and told him that Cuomo wanted to speak with him as soon as possible.

I've never spoken with the gentleman who was the Syracuse chancellor at that time, and if I ever do, I don't think I'll ask him what was going through his mind when told about this, but I think if I were running a major institution and was told that the governor wanted to speak with me immediately during a devastating blizzard, I'd assume that something horrific had happened on my campus, not that I needed to host a track meet. But by 3 p.m. on Sunday, the decision had been made to move the meet to Manley Field House on Monday, as the power in that building was expected to be back on by Sunday afternoon. My day was just beginning.

By 4 p.m., I'd been told to return to the Carrier Dome and begin to prepare for the shipment of all the track equipment back to the field house from the dome. We now had 54 inches of snow on the ground, but fortunately, it had finally stopped snowing. I broke the law by driving out of my driveway, as the state of emergency was still in effect, and I was actually pulled over by a policeman at one point during my journey back to campus. The cop clearly didn't believe me when I told him the governor had ordered me back to the Carrier Dome for a track meet, but I guess he decided who in their right mind would make up a story like that? I finally arrived at the dome to actually not see a dome, as by this point, it was totally deflated.

When I walked onto the floor of the dome, it was like being inside a tropical rainforest, as the temperature inside had to be at least 110 degrees and all the snow was melting onto the floor. If you've ever been inside an inflatable dome, you may remember that the roof is a giant grid of plastic sections. Well, each section has a plug in it, and in order to afford the water a place to go when the snow starts to melt, the plugs are undone and the water drains right onto the floor, so 287,000 square feet of surface area on top of the roof times 54 inches of snow is a significant amount of water to be draining onto a floor. Track and field equipment is very durable, as it's manufactured for outdoor usage, but high jump and pole vault pits are made out of foam rubber, and as they sat on the middle of the floor, they were essentially turned into the world's largest sponges.

The process of snow removal from the roof was a simple concept but a very difficult one on the individuals trying to accomplish the plan. Basically, the workers would go up onto the roof and into the minus-10-degree weather in one-hour shifts and shovel the snow into the low pockets where the snow was melting at its most rapid pace and then pump the water through the opened plugs and onto the floor. Long and hard work, and when a shift was up for an individual, he had to come back into the interior of the building—withstanding a 120-degree change in temperature—to help mop up the water on the floor.

By midnight, I had moved all the track and field equipment that needed to be moved to the field house down to the location of the delivery entrance of the Carrier Dome. High jump and pole vault pits, hurdles, curbing, scaffolding, starting blocks, flags, poles—you name it—had to be moved. At midnight, I was given two people to help me move the equipment, as the school couldn't afford to give me any more help, as the school's physical plant men were now getting ready to start plowing the campus, anticipating the return of 10,000 students the next day. By 5 a.m. on Monday, we had the field house set up for a track meet, but we still a little problem: The town was still in a state of emergency and none of the streets had been plowed.

At 6 a.m., as I sat in a quiet and empty field house, I heard a pounding on one of the outside doors. When I went to open it, I was shocked to see 20 men dressed in military uniforms with two of the largest snowplows I'd ever seen. I later discovered that they were airport runway snowplows. The captain of the military unit asked where he could find Brad Hackett and that the governor had sent his unit to help me out and do whatever I needed done. I hope it never happens again, but I now know that at least once in my life, the governor of a state said my name. So, I drew a map of where the hospitals were, where the hotels where the athletes were staying were, and what parking lots I thought needed to be plowed—and off they went to do what I'd asked them to do. To this day, I'm still amazed that during the largest snowstorm of the 20th century with basically the entire city of Syracuse immobile, we were able to have a track meet—with the assistance of the National Guard. In my opinion, it was ridiculous that our tax dollars were being spent for a track meet when an ambulance couldn't even pass through the majority of the streets in the city. By 11 a.m., the athletes started to file in and the meet began at noon—only two days behind schedule.

While I'd been spending the last 24 hours moving equipment and cursing my fate, I later learned that many of the athletes and coaches in town for the meet were encountering their own lifetime memories of this experience. Several of the hotels where the athletes were staying had run out of food and I was hearing from friends that people were actually hoarding the vending machines for the last bag of chips or candy bars. The meet headquarters hotel—a grand building with many beautiful ballrooms—had even allowed the athletes to work out in these rooms and apparently had also turned the Grand Ballroom of the Hotel Syracuse into an indoor track, as relay teams practiced passing batons, athletes jogged and stretched, and apparently hurdlers hurdled in the ballroom.

By Monday afternoon, the meet was running smoothly with no problems other than the field house isn't nearly as large as the Carrier Dome, so the seating capacity wasn't adequate for all the people in attendance. People were everywhere and I saw what the term "hanging from the rafters" can actually look like. But the size of the crowd added to the excitement rather than deter what could have been a rather large and disappointed group of high school athletes.

All was running smoothly—too smoothly to be exact—as close to the end of the meet, one of the athletes pulled a fire alarm. The majority of the exit doors hadn't been plowed when the National Guard had been there earlier in the day and the mass exodus of the thousands of people through one of only two plowed exits was far too slow for the now-present fire marshal. Not only was the fire department disappointed in the lack of speed of exiting the building, but it was also its understanding that the school was closed and it had been expecting an empty building when it arrived in response to the fire alarm. Clearly, the firefighters' first reaction when arriving must have been "What in the world are several thousand people doing here when no one's supposed to be out on the streets of Syracuse?"

Eventually, the meet did end, with several high school national records being broken, and I may be wrong in thinking this, but I believe that most of the athletes who endured this long and frustrating weekend ended up thinking back on it as a great adventure. Surely there were many athletes from the South and West who will look back on this weekend as the one time in their lives they experienced a blizzard. Finally, at 3 a.m. on Tuesday, I was able to go to bed—only 46 hours after having gotten up for the 5 a.m. Saturday morning conference call. Ultimately, we did the impossible: We hosted a national championship after having 54 inches of snow and a deflated roof.

My favorite postscript to the weekend is that on Tuesday afternoon, the fire marshal came into the athletic department offices with a list of too many fire code violations to count. The fire marshal was told by our athletic director that it wasn't our idea to contest the meet but rather the governor's, and if he wanted to cite anyone for the code violations, he should contact the governor. We never heard another word on the subject.

Epilogue

Well, there you have it. I think you now understand why I started this chronicle off by stating, "If all I had to do was coach." I don't think this documentation of my coaching experiences is unusual, as I've heard similar stories from the majority of my peers over the years. Whether it's vans, hotels, or equipment failures, a myriad of issues can come and go during the course of any one particular school year.

Even though I've told you the stories that rank up there with the more unusual situations that I've found myself in over the years, the bottom line is that serving as a college coach is one of the most rewarding and enjoyable occupations I can imagine.

Ninety-nine percent of the students I've been involved with over the years would never have done or been involved in anything that would warrant mention in this book and the large majority are great kids with wonderful attitudes and were a joy to be around.

I'm sure I'll continue to encounter the strange and bizarre every once in a while, but the joy and satisfaction of working with college-aged students every day and assisting them in even the slightest manner along their road to maturity is a wonderful and exciting endeavor.

This has been a wonderful journey so far, and even though the crossroads oftentimes place us in odd and frustrating situations, the path eventually provides fantastic memories. When I first started out in coaching almost 30 years ago, I never would have anticipated the path I've traversed, and in retrospect, I certainly don't think I ever would have predicted where I am now. These encounters have molded me into the person I am today and I'm quite thankful I've learned to look back and laugh about some of the more frustrating endeavors.

I just hope the next 25 years of my experience with the sport don't include quite as many stories like the ones listed on these pages, although it's certain I'll have more to tell in the future.

About the Author

Brad Hackett has been a college track and field coach for nearly 30 years. For 15 years, he was an assistant coach at the Division I level, coaching for two years at his alma mater—Colgate University—then for three years at Bucknell University and nearly 10 years at Syracuse University. Hackett has been the head track coach at Division III Muhlenberg College in Allentown, Pennsylvania, since fall 1999.

Hackett served as the triple jump chair for the men's development committee for USA Track & Field for six years and also served as the chairman of the men's development committee for USA Track & Field for seven years.

He and his wife, Lorie, reside in Schnecksville, Pennsylvania.